go as a way opens

Swanee is a hammer-swinging, Jesus-loving, storytelling, straight-shooting saint. With his wife and daughters at his side, they chose "let's do it" over "let's buy it." This decision led to many others: "let's give it" over "let's hoard it;" "let's risk it" over "let's play it safe;" "let's enter it" rather than "let's avoid it." They saw the brokenness of this world and believed they could do something about it. ~ John Stumbo, President, U. S. Christian and Missionary Alliance

Go As a Way Opens is great storytelling. Reading it was like sitting around a campfire, listening to colorful back stories of places I've grown to love in Haiti and Kenya. The people in the stories show such amazing resourcefulness, perseverance, and wit that it's no wonder Swanee and Karen loved them and found joy in serving the Lord among them. ~ Linda Adams, Director, International Child Care Ministries, Free Methodist Church

Go as a Way Opens is not for the faint of heart, but an adrenalized adventure into the way stations of human pain and need. Swanee and Karen Schwanz are two relentless pilgrims. This is a dramatic read. Just be prepared for a raucous ride. ~ Fletcher Tink, Vice President for Academic Affairs, Union University of California

This is not an ordinary story of people who have lived in tough places. This is a chronicle of people who truly believed in and lived out dependence on God. This memoir is an adventure for the reader as well. The storytelling is captivating. ~ Jo Anne Lyon, General Superintendent, The Wesleyan Church

This book is easy to read, informational, inspirational, convicting. Swanee and Karen served with total honesty and a willingness to suffer hardships. They found a way to laugh in difficult situations, to form friendships with those of very different cultures, and to learn from those they came to serve. ~ Terry Read, Missionary, Church of the Nazarene

go as a way opens

a memoir

M. L. "Swanee" Schwanz

with Keith Schwanz

Storian Press
Overland Park, Kansas

Storian Press LLC
PO Box 27112
Overland Park, KS 66225-7112
www.StorianPress.com

Cover designer: Jonathan Pelton
Typesetter: Keith Schwanz
Copyeditor: Kevin G. Smith

ISBN: 978-1-940402-06-2

Library of Congress Control Number: 2015901662

Dedication

I dedicate this book to a very special person—my wife, Karen. On June 26, 1965, nearly fifty years ago as I write this dedication, we stood before family and friends to say, "I do." And the adventure began!

Eighteen months later I proudly announced to Karen that I had just found a house we could buy. Karen's response was so kind. She turned off the stove where dinner was cooking, picked up our baby girl, and off we went the three blocks to look over the house.

The two bedroom house sat on a fifty-by-one-hundred-foot corner lot. We walked right in since the front door was off the hinges. Inside we found broken glass and rotten pumpkins recently tossed through several windows. The main level had four rooms. Trash filled the half basement. We could see that the house had potential, so within minutes we were back at our apartment calling the owner. The asking price was thirty-seven hundred dollars and Karen eagerly said, "Let's do it." This house was our home for the next fourteen months and then became our first rental property.

During our nearly twenty years outside of the United States, we often lived in less than ideal situations—taking an evening bath from a bucket, eating "different" kinds of food, sleeping in a tent for seventeen weeks while working in the Kerio Valley of Kenya. I often asked Karen to contribute so much. Seldom did she say, "Enough is enough." I remain forever grateful.

Early in our marriage Karen and I had a serious discussion about our priorities. Dozens of times we have renewed this commitment to each other. Our promise is that when given a choice between things and experiences, we will say, "let's do it" rather than, "let's buy it." Karen has been a perfect traveling companion for me. She loves people and experiences more than things that bring personal comfort.

During our seven years in Kenya, we spent much of our time installing roofs on churches in remote locations. When we finished a project and our work team was loading the tools and remaining building materials, I often walked around the job site one more time for the final inspection. Where was Karen? Likely still in the makeshift kitchen where the cooking fires continued to smolder. I would find her drinking a final cup of milk with her friends. This milk was at room temperature and smelled bad. It made a unique sound when poured into the porcelain cup because it slid out in big clumps. Since it had been mixed with charcoal dust, it took on a light gray color.

Karen definitely had the gift of hospitality in cross-cultural situations. She experienced great delight being with the wealthy European ladies in Port-au-Prince, Haiti, or drinking sour milk with toothless women in rural Kenya. Since 1978 in Haiti, I have observed that when women are comfortable socially, spiritual conversations come naturally. Karen's hospitality opened the door to deep sharing on many occasions.

Karen, you are truly the joy of my life. I delight in our "long obedience in the same direction."* To God be the glory!

Love, Swanee
December 5, 2014

P. S. *Karen, please don't ask me again to drink sour milk with you!*

---

*Friedrich Nietzsche (1844–1900)

Proceed as Way Opens:

To undertake a service or course of action without prior clarity about all the details but with confidence that divine guidance will make these apparent and assure an appropriate outcome.

~ *Faith and Practice*
Philadelphia Yearly Meeting of the
Religious Society of Friends

Contents

Foreword

On my first trip to Haiti in 1979, my brother, Swanee, and I drove from Dessalines to Port-au-Prince to meet three men coming to help us build a pastor's house. On a narrow dirt road, another driver lost control of a big truck loaded with sand and sideswiped our vehicle. Swanee jumped out and shouted in Creole, "What were you doing?" The truck driver tried to explain as we examined the damage. When we walked to the other side of the truck we saw a long skid mark on the dirt road left by the heel of the passenger's shoe. It looked like the passenger was the human brake for the heavy truck. Swanee jumped into the driver's seat of the truck and pushed the pedal all the way to the floor. No brakes. When the negotiations concluded, Swanee and the truck driver decided that a full load of sand delivered to our work site would be fair compensation for the damage to Swanee's vehicle.

One evening during that trip, Swanee and I sat on the porch of the orphanage reflecting on a productive day of work. I shared with him what I observed about how quickly he adapted to the language, the food, the culture, and the roads. Our conversation went to Ephesians 4 where the Apostle Paul discussed the vital gifts God gives to the body of Christ that "promotes the body's growth in building itself up in love" (Eph. 4:16). I witnessed God's unique gifting of my brother.

What I saw in Haiti in 1979 continued to be affirmed in the years that followed. Swanee and his wife Karen became "in-between" missionaries as they brought helpful skills not in a typical missionary's toolbox. This unique ability eventually led to the formation of GAP International, a nonprofit with the mission to "stand in the gap" (Ezek. 22:30 KJV). Swanee also had connections with willing workers who financed their own way to travel from the United States with construction teams. When God opened a way for a Swanee kind of person, Swanee stepped through the door and invited others to join him.

I'll never forget introducing Swanee to the congregation I served in Portland, Oregon. Our people had prayed for Swanee and Karen and the girls during the time of political unrest and personal risk in Haiti. As Swanee came to the podium, the congregation stood and gave him a great welcome. His opening words were typical of Swanee. "Thank you," he said. "I am not a preacher like my brother, Floyd. I am a carpenter like Jesus." The place erupted in cheers with more joyful applause.

Some of my favorite memories include multiple trips to work with Swanee in Haiti, Venezuela, Kenya, and Uganda. Our mother taught us to love and care for others, to respect and protect others, to reach out to those in need. The book you hold in your hands will take you to these places and show you these qualities through the stories of a man who led a life worthy of the calling to which he had been called (Eph. 4:1).

~ *Floyd Schwanz*

Preface

My brother, Swanee, is a storyteller. During one visit to our home in Kansas, my wife and I invited some of our friends to meet Swanee and Karen. After introductions, I announced that anyone could say a word and Swanee would tell a story. Someone said, "snake." Swanee thought for a moment, then launched into a story about an evening in Africa when some of the missionary kids saw a black mamba. That started an evening of adventure as Swanee told story after story.

Storytelling is an oral art form and uses different tools than needed when writing a narrative. Since Swanee is an oral storyteller, he used voice recognition software to digitally transcribe the stories used in this book. Some days he sent me several computer files via e-mail with thousands of words. My tasks involved discerning themes, selecting stories, organizing the stories into units with a dramatic flow, and putting it all into written form. Less than half of the stories Swanee sent ended up in the book. Early drafts went back and forth to clarify the written version of the stories. Swanee's wife, Karen, and their daughter, Shela, helped with some of the details.

We acknowledge that we struggled to nuance our discussion of race. We know that other writers have faced a similar challenge when trying to use only words to communicate ideas that touch the very core of a person. After considering various options, we chose to use terms true for the time and place of the story. For example, the Haitians often called out "blanc" (white) when Swanee walked by, so we used "white" in telling stories from Haiti. We tried substituting the word "foreigner" in one story, but that word did not sound true to the context, so we stayed with "white" even though to the contemporary ear that might not resonate well. We know that this decision could result in text deemed not appropriate by persons who may not have been in the specific context of the story that is told. We do not intend to offend anyone. We hope that our willingness to discuss issues of race furthers the awareness that God loves all people even though our words may be woefully inadequate.

Swanee and Karen lived outside of the United States and worked for faith-based organizations. Christians often use the term "missionary" to describe a person who goes into a cross-cultural setting on a religious mission. If limited to those two elements—cross-cultural and Christian mission—then Swanee and Karen might be thought of as missionaries.

But there is another aspect of missionary that must be considered. Most definitions of missionary include the fact that a person is "sent" on the religious mission. Luke reported that the church in Antioch prayed for Paul and Barnabas, laid hands on them as an act of consecration, and "sent them off" (Acts 13:3). These early missionaries were released from and impelled into service by the Antioch congregation.

If being sent makes a missionary, the term would not apply to Swanee and Karen. Their home congregation did not send them to serve in Haiti or Kenya, although many of their friends supported them in a multitude of ways. Swanee talked with pastors and denominational leaders about his aware-ness of God's direction, but these leaders never sent him. So Swanee's life has little in common with the "sent-ness" of Paul and Barnabas's experience with the Antioch congregation.

But what happened to Paul on his second missionary journey provides a different image. While in Troas, "During the night Paul had a vision: there stood a man of Macedonia pleading with him and saying, 'Come over to Macedonia and help us'" (Acts 16:9). The man summoned Paul, urged him to respond, and called him to cross the Aegean Sea to work with him. Since Paul understood that the man spoke for God, Paul followed the vision.

Swanee and Karen lived this story. People outside of the United States invited them to become partners in the global mission. These were people who knew Swanee and Karen, knew their motivation, and knew the skills they freely offered. They accepted the invitations as they were able. The more they responded, the more opportunities they had and the more others in the United States became partners in supporting their work. Swanee and Karen were called by those already in another country, never sent by those in the United States.

We find the Holy Spirit's action in both of these stories about Paul. In the first, the action of the visionary Antioch congregation served as a tangible expression that Paul and Barnabas were actually "sent out by the Holy Spirit" (Acts 13:4). In the vision in which the Macedonian man pleaded with Paul to cross the sea, Paul became "convinced that God had called" (Acts 16:10).

As you will see in the stories in this book, Swanee and Karen were convinced that God directed their decisions. They set off on journeys when they did not fully understand what lay ahead. They took steps that seemed silly to some and faced hindrances that at times felt insurmountable. But they lived in confidence that God would continue to guide and that good things would emerge from their efforts. You will read descriptions of those discernments, obstacles, and triumphs in the stories in this book.

This is a memoir, not an autobiography. As such, it focuses on about fifteen years, not a lifetime. A majority of the stories come from only two of the countries in which Swanee worked, Haiti and Kenya. A few themes intertwine throughout the memoir; some personal information expected in an autobiography is omitted. The book follows a basic chronology, but the themes are more important than the timeline, so we jump around a bit.

The stories are told from Swanee's perspective as he remembers the experiences. We intend to tell the stories straight, but in the end the *feeling of the memory* leads the way. That is how a memoir works. On occasion we use dialogue to tell part of the story. These conversations were recreated as remembered and should not be read as exact quotes.

Swanee speaks to the partnership with his wife Karen in the Dedication. You should assume Karen's involvement even if her name is not mentioned in a particular telling of a story. Their daughters, Shela and Sher'ri, played a key role at many junctures and the hundreds of people on short-term mission teams who worked with Swanee had influence. Swanee mentions these persons in the Acknowledgments but they do not necessarily show up in the stories.

As I lived with these stories during the writing process, I began to see common threads woven throughout. In this memoir you will find many stories about responding to those who suffer. Often it involved physical suffering. Sometimes the suffering came because the social system disadvantaged persons or those with power used it against others.

Swanee's response often involved care for the person who suffered. I have heard him talk for years about the word "compassion." The prefix *com-* means "with," so compassion is to feel *with* the person who suffers, to share the suffering. One story invites you to ignore the nauseating smell and walk beside a teenager suffering with cancer that ate away his nose. Another story bids you to sit in the car and listen to the utter anguish of a mother of four who just learned she had AIDS.

In other stories you will find Swanee seeking to empower people who suffer. He equipped and encouraged those treated unfairly, those disadvantaged by corruption or neglect. Stories in this book will introduce you to Francine in Dessalines, Haiti, first as a laborer, then as a contractor after Swanee provided him with tools. In other stories you will hear several men in Africa refer to Swanee as "Dad." These young men learned to be better workers, husbands, and fathers as Swanee equipped and empowered them.

Another thread woven through the stories shows how Swanee served as a liaison between those who suffered and those who relieved suffering. As a builder, this most often came through what nonprofit organizations call "increasing capacity."

For persons living in long-term relationships with those who suffer, Swanee's work increased their capacity to compassionately respond to needs. We do not tell all of the stories in this book, but Swanee worked on hospitals and clinics in La Gonâve, Dessalines, and Port-au-Prince, Haiti; Bomet, Kenya; and Kampala, Uganda. Through stories, you will walk the halls and watch as healthcare workers care for the infirm. Swanee helped make it easier for them to provide compassionate care.

For members of short-term mission teams, Swanee and Karen served as a bridge over which persons available for a couple of weeks contributed to the empowerment of those who suffer. Stories will describe providing local congregations with better space in which to gather for discipleship and worship and empowering children and young adults through the construction of school buildings.

In story after story, you will discover that hospitality formed the primary means through which Swanee and Karen cared for those who suffered and facilitated those who relieved suffering. In its most basic sense, hospitality involves making room for another person. Hospitality is relational, coming alongside of someone, and this may or may not involve getting out the finest dishes and the linen napkins to serve tea and cookies. Through story, you will lay down the tools for a bit to talk with a man who just had his right leg amputated above the knee. You will sit in the dark night in northern Kenya and listen to a lonely Kipsigis missionary living among the Pokot people as an incarnational expression of God's love.

When short-term mission teams came to visit, Swanee and Karen invited them to use the space already opened through hospitality. Swanee and Karen nurtured relationships with diverse people in Kericho, Kenya, for example, and invited team members from the United States to join them in that open, gracious space. Swanee and Karen established friendships with Muslims and Hindus and used these relationships to encourage reconciliation. Through story, you will discover that diverse people can come together for the common good.

At times, Swanee served those who suffered as an advocate with those who caused or prolonged the suffering and those with the power to bring about change. On numerous occasions Swanee had the courage to confront injustice with the perpetrators of that injustice. In story, you will duck as the gravel flies behind the spinning tires of the Mercedes carrying the angry "big man" following a failed shake down. A story will compel you to stand shoulder to shoulder with Swanee as he denounced the sexual violence of a forty-year-old man against a twelve-year-old girl.

The best stories will cause you to look away from the page, even for a moment, so you can reflect on the implications of what you just read.

Insight and wisdom emerge when the imagination fully engages in story. Abstract concepts spring to life in story. Story weaves into one cloth experiences that seem chaotic and disconnected, and does so in a way that captivates even the most easily-distracted person. Story stirs the emotions: the laughter of delight, the groan of anguish, the sigh of despair, the whisper of love. Story sparks a vision and fans the flame until people burn with passion. Folks from various cultural contexts and experiences come together through story. Story helps articulate *what is* so that by putting the collective shoulder to the task people can bend *what will be* toward a better trajectory.

Nancy Mellon wrote, "Although setbacks of all kinds may discourage us, the grand old process of storytelling puts us in touch with strengths we may have forgotten, with wisdom that has faded or disappeared, and with hopes that have fallen into darkness."

Strength. Wisdom. Hopes. May the power of story refocus within you a clear vision and re-energize you with courage to engage with others for the common good.

~ Keith Schwanz

Acknowledgments

Years ago I spoke to about one hundred fifty people on a Sunday night in an attempt to recruit a second team to go to southern Mexico. After I had shown eighty slides about the project and the lights were turned up, I asked if anyone had a question. A hand went up in the middle of the congregation. A man of about sixty stood to ask a three-part question. "Are you suggesting I take my vacation, pay all of my own expenses, and work for nothing?"

For just a moment I found humor in his question, but I did not break a smile. I simply said, "Yes. Yes. Yes." Before the man sat down, he said, "I thought that was what you were getting at." I am sorry that I never saw that man again.

But there were more than eighteen hundred Americans who bought airplane tickets to come work with us. Together we made great memories in some very remote locations. The stories in this book show what can be accomplished through a team effort, that suffering can be relieved and those who serve can be equipped to better assist.

Karen and I provided free labor to help construct about two hundred fifty buildings, but there were costs involved. We owe a huge debt to our family and friends who gave time, prayers, and dollars so we could represent them on the front line. In many ways we were like an extended family. We will remain forever committed to our family and friends who were our partners.

My Mom and Dad—Myrtle and Leroy Schwanz—passed on the DNA of service to my siblings and me. For many years my sister, Phyllis, kept the GAP International books and carefully cared for our personal finances while we were out of the country. My older brother, Floyd, served on the initial board of directors for GAP International and joined us on several work projects. My younger brother, Keith, serves on the current GAP board and assisted with writing this book. I am blessed because volunteerism is in the Schwanz DNA.

The first time we went to Haiti our daughters, Shela and Sher'ri, were twelve and ten years old. We were in Haiti for a few weeks that summer, then had a six-month stay the next year. Eventually we moved to Haiti and lived there while both girls attended high school. Part of our motivation involved wanting them to live in another culture, but those years did more than just give the girls a cross-cultural experience. The time in Haiti shaped Shela and Sher'ri so that even today they are like human magnets that pull people towards God. Some of the stories in this book show the influence they had on the decisions I made.

Writing a book takes months of work and cannot be completed without the involvement of many people. I especially want to thank those who served as the "first readers": Grant Christy, Gary Metzgar, Jon Pelton, Floyd Schwanz, Judi Schwanz, and Sharon Templeman. These persons helped us identify places that needed attention in the revision process. I also thank Kevin Smith (copyediting), Jon Twitchell (proofreading), and Jon Pelton (cover design) for their assistance.

I gratefully acknowledge the contributions of many people who were part of the stories I tell in this memoir. I am a better man because of these key relationships.

Chapter 1

An Extended Hand

The better the day, the better the deed.
~ Honduran Proverb

Hurricane Fifi devastated Honduras in September 1974. Winds in excess of one hundred thirty miles per hour and torrential rains hammered the desperate people of this Central American country. Buses used for evacuation spun out on mountain passes. Mud slides formed earthen dams that, for a while, held the water cascading down the mountainsides, only to unleash massive avalanches of water when the dams disintegrated. Flash floods toppled thousands of houses and isolated hundreds of villages. Fifi is the fourth most deadly hurricane on record with eight to ten thousand fatalities.

Ray, an associate pastor at our church, immediately organized a team to go to Honduras to assist with the disaster response and to help begin the rebuilding process. I joined the team for what was my first international trip.

In Honduras, we personally saw the raw power of wind and water. We saw water marks seven feet up the walls of the house we repaired. The raging water turned uprooted trees into battering rams that smashed everything in its path. People simply vanished, families left to grieve without knowing the fate of loved ones.

We also witnessed the strength of people during times of terrible adversity. During the Sunday worship service, we heard the compelling story of a woman, perhaps forty years old. She was short, maybe five feet tall. A flash flood washed away her house about midnight. The raging current pushed her against a large tree, so she grabbed a branch and held on. Her survival depended on it. She heard cries for help, but in the darkness could not see who called out. Simply reacting to what she heard, the woman caught a child by the hair and somehow mustered the strength to hang on to the tree with one arm and pull the child close with the other. Only then did she realize that she fought with the torrent to save her own ten-year-old daughter.

As I listened to the testimony, I tried to imagine myself in this woman's situation: utter darkness, water current yanking against my grip, constant strain sapping my strength. What intense fear she must have experienced. I wondered if I would let go with one hand to save another person. *Would I give up half of my security to try to rescue a person calling out in the darkness? But what if I refused to reach out? Could I live with myself if I did not extend a hand to help?* The conversation with myself that started on that Sunday morning continued for many weeks.

Near the end of our time in Honduras, I went to the job site in the haze of first light, just before the sun rose that morning. I wanted to get an early start because I needed to spread adhesive for the countertops and wanted to avoid the dust from other workers. As I walked to work that morning, I passed a tent village where many lived after losing their houses. I looked at embers already glowing, a cooking pot sitting on three stones over an open fire. At that moment I became aware of the sting of poverty like never before. I wept as I walked alone. I always thought people lived in poverty because of laziness. But these people were not slothful or sluggish. I looked around and could see how much my new friends suffered. I had lived with them for a week and knew that laziness did not contribute to their distress.

That trip to Honduras changed the direction of my life. For the first time I stood face to face with extreme poverty and suffering. And I discovered the joy of intentional action to alleviate misery and distress. Almost imperceptible at the time, my grip loosened on the things I expected to provide security. I began to extend my hand to those who suffered.

Just a few days before we flew to Honduras in 1974, Pastor Ray designated me as the project team leader. I did not want that responsibility. I happily joined the team, but I accepted the leadership assignment reluctantly. At the end of the trip, however, everyone seemed to feel good about what they had contributed to the project. I had taken the initial steps on a new journey as a facilitator of short-term mission teams.

As I look back over the decades since that trip to Honduras, I recognize that at no time did I possess a master plan for my life. In 1974, I could not anticipate the rich experiences that would come my way or the rewarding relationships just waiting for my arrival. In a sense, the building of my life occurred without blueprints. Instead, to shift the metaphor, the road before me became evident one moment at a time. Step by step I discerned the way forward. The key element, I discovered, involved my willingness to take the next step.

Chapter 2

Overflow

What I need I also must give.

~ Haitian Proverb

The importance of January 24, 1978, became evident only years later. My brother, Floyd, told me about Teen Mission International. Intrigued, Karen and I drove to Seattle for a meeting in which Teen Mission representatives talked about the ministry and the need for team leaders the following summer.

The project that caught my attention was at an orphanage in Haiti. I very clearly remember hearing about rats that had eaten the ears of small children in their sleep. The story tugged at my heart. I recognized those feelings since I experienced a similar thing in Honduras.

Karen and I slept in the basement of the church building of the congregation that hosted the Teen Mission meeting. As was my practice in those days, before going to sleep I opened my Bible to read from Proverbs. Since it was the twenty-fourth day of the month, I read from Proverbs 24. "Rescue those who are unjustly sentenced to death; don't stand back and let them die. Don't try to disclaim responsibility by saying you didn't know about it. For God, who knows all hearts, knows yours, and he knows you knew! And he will reward everyone according to his deeds" (Prov. 24:11–12 TLB).

My mind immediately connected the description we heard of the living conditions of orphans in Haiti in the twentieth century with the wisdom of Solomon more than nine hundred years before Christ. The ancient words had immediate connection in my life. Before leaving Seattle, we told the Teen Mission staff that we would lead a team of teenagers doing construction at the orphanage in Haiti.

One of the reasons we felt free to make this commitment came directly from the settlement of a lawsuit the day before our trip to Seattle. In the previous months, dozens of times we walked in and out of attorney offices trying to settle a liability claim by a man who lived in a three-unit apartment building we owned. About the time it looked like we could wrap up the issue, something else came along that needed resolution. For two and a half years the case dragged on.

We also worked on constructing for ourselves a new house situated on three acres of prime real estate. The lawsuit caused the bank to reject our loan application. The bank officer with whom we made the application finally found a way for us to get the funds we needed to complete the construction. All of this had been a heavy load that, when lifted, allowed us to listen with clarity to the voices of God and God's people. We decided to spend the summer in Haiti, the first work trip for Karen, Shela, and Sher'ri.

I went to my boss at the construction company where I worked and told him that I needed the summer off. The boss's response did not encourage me. Some on the construction crew thought I had gone crazy for religion, a conversation that continued for many weeks. In the end, the boss fired me, or maybe I quit. Either way, I did not have a job or health insurance. My decision to spend the summer with a group of teenagers in Haiti put the financial well-being of my family at risk.

We met our team at the Teen Mission boot camp in Florida. Our team consisted of thirty-four teenagers, ages thirteen to nineteen, three college-age assistant leaders, and the four of us. The director of the Haitian orphanage joined us at the boot camp for a few days as he traveled back to Haiti after being with his ill father for three months.

Teen Mission required that all team members wear boots all summer, so we literally gathered at boot camp. Team leaders had training on how to feed the team. When you do the math, we had almost five thousand meals to prepare and serve. We had basic orientation to skills needed in construction. We spent time on the obstacle course working together to move everyone to the finish line on the other side of a Florida swamp. Teams preparing to go to various places in the world contended with each other in an attempt to bring each team together as a cohesive unit. It seemed to foster a sense of competition between the teams rather than camaraderie. When we left the boot camp, in my briefcase I carried forty-one airplane tickets, cash for building materials, cash for land travel, and cash for food. I had been the project leader in Honduras, but the weight of responsibility for this team felt heavier.

We traveled by plane to Haiti, then in an open cattle truck to Dessalines. When we arrived, it felt like we reached the end of the road. We soon discovered that none of the twenty thousand people living in Dessalines had electricity or telephone service. At that time there were only six cars in the town. Mail came whenever someone went to Port-au-Prince to get it.

When we arrived at the Ebenezer Glenn Orphanage, we scouted out the compound where ten adult workers cared for forty-two orphans. As we got settled, we set up the tents in which we would sleep for the next five weeks. Another Teen Mission team stayed with us the first night; the next morning they traveled five more hours to Cap-Haïtien, the location of their summer project.

While Karen organized the pancake breakfast on our first morning, I walked around the four-acre compound. I looked at the existing buildings, seeking to learn what I could about construction methods. The orphans slept in a dormitory about thirty by sixty feet. The compound included a small clinic, a small building they used for food preparation, and a four-hole outhouse. The directors lived in a house on the property.

I found the location of our primary project. I inspected the concrete foundation in place for a thirty-by-sixty-foot building that the orphanage would use for food storage and as a dining hall. Children would sit at small picnic tables for meals in this building when completed.

Many questions flooded my mind as I walked the grounds. *Where do we get water? Where will the forty-one persons on our team sit to have meals together? How do we bathe? How can I keep teenagers busy so they stay out of trouble? What have I done to my family by bringing them to this place?* I realize now that I was in the throes of culture shock.

As I walked around with these questions storming through my mind, I heard Sher'ri say, "Pa fe sa."

"What did you just say?" I asked her.

"Pa fe sa," she repeated. "Dad, speaking Creole is easy. Just listen to them and repeat what they say." Sher'ri had celebrated her tenth birthday just a few days before.

Very quickly both of our daughters were speaking Creole. They learned the art of putting tight braids in crisp black hair. When I saw my girls carrying Haitian orphans on their hips and chattering away in Creole, I began to relax. My daughters got acclimated to a new culture faster than I did. They helped me believe that I could make the adjustment too.

Because Don, the orphanage director, had just returned to Dessalines from being in the United States for three months, no building materials had been purchased or delivered to the site as planned. So I spent the rest of that first full day with Don creating a list of materials and tools we would need to construct the dining hall. Early the next morning the two of us started the four-hour trip to Port-au-Prince. By early afternoon we had paid for concrete blocks, cement, lumber, roofing materials, nails, paint, and a few tools. With receipts in hand, we began our search for a truck we could hire to transport the materials to Dessalines.

We stopped by a mission campus outside of Port-au-Prince hoping that their gray truck and a driver might be available for the trip to Dessalines. The first missionary we saw asked Don if he had called the United States. Don did not know anything about needing to make a telephone call. Since the orphanage in Dessalines did not have telephone service, Don's family had called missionaries in Port-au-Prince hoping somehow to get a message to Don. The missionary informed my new friend that his father had died.

Don quickly made several decisions. We would drive back to Dessalines that day as planned. He would return to Port-au-Prince with a suitcase and his passport the next morning to fly to the United States for his father's funeral. He told me that I would be in charge of the construction for the next four weeks while he was gone. His wife, Doris, would stay with us, but I needed to do all of the construction tasks. He handed me a canvas bag full of cash and taught me to count Haitian currency.

The more I thought about the deteriorating situation, the greater the urgency that swept over me. In less than twenty-four hours I would be on my own in a place I did not know nor understand. The fact that the orphanage did not have the building materials was the first hitch in the plans for the summer. Now my primary link with the culture would not be available. I saw the potential of a flash flood.

The two of us stopped at a fast-food restaurant for takeaway chicken, then started the trip home. As we drove, Don told stories about his father. He told me that he had been criticized by some people for not staying in the United States to care for his father, but that would have required six years away from the orphanage. I wondered if the three months he had just spent with his father was an attempt to respond to the shame imposed on him by those critical comments. He sang hymns as he drove on the rough Haitian roads. In those moments I recognized that Don was preparing to bury his father.

A stillness covered the orphanage compound when we arrived. Everyone was asleep. A brief honk of the car horn aroused the watchman who opened the iron gate for us.

As we unpacked the old blue Chevy Suburban, I handed the watchman the two food boxes with the chicken bones and a few French fries. Before going to my tent, I saw the watchman eating the last of the chicken bones. Crunch, crunch, crunch. He ate everything. I did not know that some people were hungry enough to eat something like that.

I went to bed dead tired, but sleep did not come.

Very early the next morning, Don left for the United States. Keeping teenagers busy on the construction of a building lay squarely on my shoulders. I had to find my way in a new culture with only a few hours of orientation.

I organized our team and we began to construct the building. With some teens mixing mortar and others laying blocks, we made good progress. I soon became aware that we could finish the building two weeks before we were scheduled to leave Haiti. This posed a serious problem, so I looked for other things our team could do. We gathered rocks scattered on the ground inside the fences surrounding the orphanage to use in restoring roads. We repaired fences, trimmed trees, and painted other buildings. I kept rotating teens among the various tasks mostly because no one likes to pick up rocks all day.

I discovered that one landmark in Haiti is the Citadel, a large mountaintop fortress in northern Haiti near Cap-Haïtien. I arranged for transportation and we spent a day climbing to the top for a picturesque view.

While on this sightseeing trip, we stopped to visit with the Teen Mission team that spent the first night with us. Right away I recognized that this team faced a difficult situation. The orphanage compound consisted of several small buildings and appeared to operate with little funding. The toilets were not adequately maintained. Rats (more than one) ran behind my bare butt while sitting on the outdoor toilet. The children were dirty and poorly dressed. It seemed like the kids were just one step ahead of being on the streets. Further, the team had poured the concrete floor for their project, but they had yet to start laying the blocks. "We have no idea what we are doing," the team leader confessed.

When I returned to Dessalines, I decided to do something in addition to praying. I gathered our team and proposed that they elect four persons to go with me to Cap-Haïtien. The five of us left early one morning on public transportation for the five-hour trip. When we arrived, I told the teenagers with me to wait outside. If we were not welcomed, we would go back to Dessalines that same day. When I walked into the orphanage, no one was working on the construction project. I offered our assistance, they received us, and we stayed three days working with them. The teens from our team provided enough leadership to get the other team going. When we heard their report after arriving back at the Teen Mission camp in Florida, they told us that they finished the roof with the car lights on for illumination. They did it! We rejoiced with them.

At the debriefing sessions in Florida, I was told that I broke the rules by taking teenagers from one team to assist another team. I did not receive the reprimand well. I gave up my summer. I made my employer angry with me and did not have a job when I returned home. I managed thirty-four teens in difficult living conditions. We finished our project early. We did everything expected of us . . . and more. And I was being chastised for helping another team?

"I did the right thing," I said. "We provided enough help to the other team that they succeeded when it looked like failure was inevitable. And we showed our team the joy of serving." I am not sure my speech convinced anyone. Rules that prolong the pain of those who suffer should be broken, so I would do the same thing again if necessary.

Karen developed a process through which she met individually with each team member. The orphanage had only one refrigerator, a kerosene-powered unit. Our team could put two bottles of soda in the refrigerator at a time. Mid-morning and mid-afternoon, Karen met with individuals to share a soda. Teen Mission wisely sent each team out with a library of about twenty-five books. In the first meeting with Karen, the teen selected a book from the library. At the second meeting they discussed the book as they enjoyed the cold drink together.

The discussions went far beyond the content of the books. Teenagers talked with Karen about fragmented families. Some described substance abuse and sexual harassment. Karen and I began to pray for God to use our time with these teenagers to bring healing and wholeness.

Very early one morning, with Don still in the United States for his father's funeral, people came to the orphanage with twins who appeared to be only a day or two old. Doris feared that the newborns had spinal meningitis, so she committed to drive the girls to the Albert Schweitzer Hospital about an hour and a half away. She asked Karen to travel with her to care for the babies while she drove. Karen held one child, then the other, praying that they would reach the hospital in time.

When they arrived, each woman took a child and walked into the hospital. Karen walked past sick people lying on the sidewalk and in the hallway. Some laid in vomit and diarrhea.

Karen held one baby while the doctor did the examination. With the infant on Karen's lap, the doctor did a spinal tap. Both babies died shortly afterwards.

Karen expected ceramic tile, clean floors, bright lights, and clean sheets on the beds. Instead she found a hospital that was understaffed and underfunded. They did not even have an examination table, so she held a dying child on her lap and watched the spinal tap.

On the way back to Dessalines, Karen said, "I'm not sure I'll ever be the same again."

"I pray to God that that is true," Doris replied.

At summer's end, I wondered if the men with whom I worked in Oregon were correct after all. A construction worker needs to take advantage of the summer season when the "big money" comes easily. But I had fulfilled the commitment I made the previous January; at least I did that right. In our five weeks in Dessalines we had lived in tents like Abraham, worked like Nehemiah, complained like the children of Israel, and trusted God like David, sometimes hot, sometimes cold. The boiling, humid weather had sapped my strength. With a large team of teenagers plus the orphans all living in a small space, I did not have any privacy. As the team leader, I had no down time or days off. I was more than ready to go home.

There were four Christian churches in Dessalines, so we went to a different church on the first four Sundays of that summer trip. On our final Sunday, we let everyone on the Teen Mission team choose which congregation to visit a second time.

Our family decided to worship with the Church of the Nazarene congregation. As we walked about a mile, I thought about the next Sunday when I would drive to my local congregation in my air-conditioned station wagon. The service would be about one hour long, not two and a half hours. I would sit on a comfortable pew, not on a wooden bench in a hot, tin-roofed building. I longed for organ music and quiet reverence, not what seemed to me to be noisy chaos. My missionary adventure was about to end and I was oh so ready. In just a few hours I would start the journey home to electric lights, hot showers, and clean toilets.

When we arrived at the church, they ushered the "guests" to the front row. Since we had no way to wiggle out of the service early, I settled in for the duration.

The worship leader suggested a contest between the men and women to see who could contribute the largest offering. This seemed ridiculous to me in my state of mind. *What a waste of time*, I thought.

The women went first. When they collected all they could, they counted the offering and announced the total. Then the women sang a victory song. When the men had received and counted their offering, they had collected more than the women. The hot building filled with laughter. They called on the men to sing their victory song. The women begged the worship leader for permission to receive another offering, which the worship leader foolishly allowed (in my humble, sweaty opinion). When the women surpassed the men's total, they started singing again. The men took another offering and were eventually declared the winners.

I was tired. I wanted to get back to the orphanage for lunch and a nap.

Don sat next to me on the front row of this church. "How much did they receive in the offering?" I asked.

"In the final offering of the men, or the total offering?"

"The total," I said. "How much for all four offerings?"

"Two dollars and eighty-five cents."

I looked around at the one hundred fifty Christians singing and dancing with joy. *They rejoice for an offering of $2.85?!*

Just as the pastor began his sermon, we heard the sound of singing coming from the road. I looked outside and saw a large cattle truck with about thirty people standing in the back. A neighboring congregation had come to worship with us that morning. Laughter filled the air as the guests walked into the church. People greeted each other with hugs.

The pastor welcomed the visitors, and then said to his congregation that since the guests had traveled thirty-five miles, the congregation needed to receive a love offering to help them with their expenses. Offering number five! I counted. Testimonies and singing followed the offering. Again we prepared for the sermon.

A Bible school student traveled with the thirty people. To my dismay, they asked him to bring the morning message. *Why, Lord? Not a student who does not even know how to preach!* I felt trapped in a front row seat. At my home church, the good reverend doctor would never ask a visitor, let alone a student, to preach. I was tired of the laughter, tired of the mass confusion. I wanted out.

Since the preacher spoke in Creole, I asked Don, "What scripture is the student using for the sermon?"

"Second Corinthians, chapter eight," came the reply.

I opened my Bible and began to read. "Now I want to tell you what God in his grace has done for the churches in Macedonia. Though they have been going through much trouble and hard times, they have mixed their wonderful joy with their deep poverty, and the result has been an overflow of giving to others" (2 Cor. 8:1–2 TLB).

I began weeping.

"They gave not only what they could afford but far more; and I can testify that they did it because they wanted to and not because of nagging on my part. They begged us to take the money so they could share in the joy of helping the Christians in Jerusalem" (2 Cor. 8:3–4 TLB).

I thought to myself, *the student had no idea the congregation had received four offerings prior to his arrival. He did not know what had been going through my mind.*

"Best of all, they went beyond our highest hopes, for their first action was to dedicate themselves to the Lord and to us, for whatever directions God might give to them through us. They were so enthusiastic about it that we have urged Titus, who encouraged your giving in the first place, to visit you and encourage you to complete your share in this ministry of giving" (2 Cor. 8:5–6 TLB).

I was a mess, sitting on the front row with no way of escape. That young student preached his heart out and I sat weeping. I did not understand what he said in Creole, but the Holy Spirit spoke to me through the scriptures.

I kept thinking about $2.85 and the congregation's laughter in giving. *Why do poor people enjoy giving?* As the preacher continued, I read and re-read 2 Corinthians 8.

"Of course, I don't mean that those who receive your gifts should have an easy time of it at your expense, but you should divide with them. Right now you have plenty and can help them; then at some other time they can share with you when you need it. In this way, each will have as much as he needs. Do you remember what the Scriptures say about this? 'He that gathered much had nothing left over, and he that gathered little had enough.' So you also should share with those in need" (2 Cor. 8:13–15 TLB).

I thought about the primitive living conditions of the previous five weeks and about my new house on three acres on the south side of Bull Mountain in Oregon. I do not recall ever asking God to help me understand the meaning of the verses that I read from 2 Corinthians 8 that morning. I knew what they meant.

Chapter 3

A Pitcher Pump

A fair deal does not spoil a friendship.
~ Haitian Proverb

The day after we returned to Oregon following the summer in Haiti with Teen Mission, I started looking for work. I went to my former employer, the one I left on less than ideal terms, and asked if they needed any carpenters. The boss replied, "I'm always looking for someone who is good. Come to work tomorrow." I was grateful to have a job.

Our family settled into our typical routine: school, work, church. Over the next few months, fourteen of the teenagers on our Teen Mission team wrote to us about how transformational the summer had been for them. Karen and I rejoiced at the testimonies to changed lives.

In those days, Karen taught the junior high Sunday school class for our local congregation. Given our experience with Teen Mission, we began to dream about taking a group of teens from our church to the Ebenezer Glenn Orphanage the next summer. When we wrote to see if such a trip might be possible, Don and Doris immediately responded to ask us to stay for six months. They had not been back to the United States as a family for seven years. Each family member had returned from time to time, but they had not been able to get away from their responsibilities at the orphanage so that everyone could travel together. We began working toward that goal.

I never knew this until much later, but at first Karen did not want to return to Dessalines for the six months. She willingly considered taking a team in for a couple of weeks, but not moving there for six months. She intuitively felt that this decision signaled a major life turn. She told a small group of women in a Bible study that it was not just for six months, but that everything would change. She did not want to make that transition, so she argued with God. I never saw it, but she intensely struggled with the decision. One day while she stood at the kitchen sink in our dream house looking over the valley, she realized that if she felt absolutely miserable in her resistance that maybe stepping through the door as it opened would bring peace. In that moment she said, "Yes, Lord." She looked back on that experience as her sanctification, of being fully consecrated to God's will and empowered for holy service. As it turned out, her insight about the six months signaling a shift in our lives proved true.

I sold the three-unit apartment building, the one for which I settled the liability lawsuit prior to going to Haiti the first time. The ten thousand dollar profit from that sale would support us for the six months in Dessalines.

I had only been back at work a short time when I went to my boss to tell him that I would be gone from mid-June through the end of December. To my surprise, the boss received the announcement well. He even offered to keep the family on the health insurance plan while we were gone. Something had changed. We went to the school our daughters attended. The teachers provided books and materials that the girls could study on their own. They would then be ready to rejoin their classmates the next January. The youth pastor from our church agreed to rent our furnished house while we were gone. Everything fell into place quite easily.

We made arrangements for a work team from our congregation to visit us in Haiti. My brother, Floyd, organized a second team to build a parsonage. On this trip Floyd and I sat on the porch talking one evening about what he observed in my adjustment to a new culture (see the Foreword).

On our wedding anniversary, June 26, 1979, we returned to Haiti. The weather was stormy that day. After going through immigration and customs, we loaded our luggage into Don's car. We stopped for lunch at a restaurant in downtown Port-au-Prince. Once inside the restaurant it began to rain like crazy. Don said, "On days like this I've seen cars washed into the ocean with the flooding water." That seemed like an exaggeration to me until I started seeing the road in front of the restaurant fill with water. Runoff from the mountains used the streets as channels to the ocean. Baskets and wooden chairs drifted by. I saw a dog swimming frantically to find high ground. Just as my friend suggested could happen, a car without a driver slowly floated past the restaurant window. Several men in short pants sloshed through the water to guide this floating car against a big tree and save it from drifting into the ocean just one hundred yards away. The adventure had started.

The following day we drove to Dessalines and began the orientation on keeping an orphanage running smoothly. We expected to have two weeks with the orphanage directors coaching us, but about three days into the process our friends told us they would leave the next Tuesday. At that point we had only three more days to learn how to care for the children and handle the orphanage business. On Monday we drove back to Port-au-Prince and learned where to buy medicine, food, cheap shoes, auto parts, and other items to run the orphanage. About noon on Tuesday we said goodbye to our friends.

Our family of four watched the green and white DC-3 airplane until it disappeared in the blue sky. Standing alone, I had an empty feeling in my gut. So many questions remained unanswered. *Could we really survive for six months? What if? What if? What if?*

Karen and I were ill prepared . . . and we knew it. Our girls were thirteen and eleven years old, much too young to share our insecurities, so we put on a happy face. We had no friends to visit in Port-au-Prince, so we did what Americans do; we went shopping. We stopped at a grocery store to buy food, and then bought ice cream cones before beginning the four-hour drive to Dessalines.

Karen took primary responsibility for keeping the orphanage functioning. Ten Haitian workers assisted and Karen managed the payroll. With all the orphans and workers, it seemed like every day someone needed medical care, so Karen read the healthcare books and did what she could to treat them. We had two work teams and other visitors during this time for whom Karen provided wonderful hospitality.

I took care of maintenance issues at the orphanage, but most of my attention focused beyond the orphanage walls. I visited the pastors of the four congregations in town and offered my assistance.

I worked with the Baptists first. I repaired twelve steps going into the church building. I did not spend much money on this job, just bought two sacks of cement and some sand and paid a few workers. This job helped me start making friends in Dessalines.

My next project consisted of helping the Church of God. At that point, they had constructed the walls of a large church building, but the walls appeared too weak to support the roof. I suggested that we install pillars to support the walls. About every eight feet along the sides of the building, and on both sides of the front door, we dug down to where we could build

41

footers on solid soil. This project did not cost much, maybe five hundred dollars, but investing a little bit paid off since many years later I returned to Dessalines to see that the building still stood.

The Free Methodist project required a larger investment. This congregation used its sanctuary as a school during the week. About four hundred fifty children and eight teachers crowded into the one room. I could not understand how anyone learned anything with all the noise and activity. To make things more difficult, at every window children outside stood looking in, wishing they had the opportunity to attend school.

On one trip to Port-au-Prince, the first in three weeks, I picked up groceries, building materials, and mail. As I sat in that old rusted truck parked in front of the post office, I opened an envelope from our neighbor in Oregon, an acquaintance, not a longtime friend. He had enclosed a check for a large amount. I laughed and wept as I looked at the check in my hand. I could hardly wait to get back to Dessalines. We would build classrooms for the Free Methodist school.

When I told the Free Methodist pastor the good news, he said, "My teachers have been grumpy this year. We have too many students inside. We have been praying for help, but we expected it *next year*. I must go tell them that God answered our prayers *this year*."

I will never forget the excitement on the first day of construction. Men cleared the land with machetes and dug the footers with picks and shovels. Women and children carried rocks down from the mountain on their heads that we would use for the foundation. It was a hot day to do this type of work.

Earlier that day I watched the town butcher pull pork out of a five-gallon bucket and drop it into three kettles. The meat looked gray. The butcher said that he wanted to cook it before the meat went bad. I thought it was already beyond safe to eat. The "cooking down" process created an awful smell and the heat of the fires added to our discomfort as we worked nearby. But even that irritation did not tamp down our buoyant spirits.

Shortly before noon, I was down in the ditch taking my turn at digging the footers. Because the clay soil hung to the rocks, it required a lot of effort to excavate using hand tools. As I straightened up to catch my breath, I noticed one of the teachers watching us. He was nicely dressed, clean, healthy. He had one long fingernail, the Haitian way of letting people know a person's status as being educated and too sophisticated for manual labor.

"Why aren't you down in the ditch?" I asked.

"I get paid for teaching school, not digging ditches," he said. He stood still, the quiet center of attention.

None of those who heard this exchange said anything. No one moved. Everyone waited silently. All I could hear was the boiling water in the three kettles nearby.

After a long pause, I asked, "Who was the greatest teacher the world has ever known?"

After several moments, the teacher said, "Jesus."

"And who was the first and greatest Christian missionary?" I continued.

Again, silence. "Paul," he finally replied.

"Are you greater than Jesus or Paul?"

The stillness started feeling painful. The teacher looked at me. "I don't understand," he said.

With the pastor's assistance, we explained to everyone listening that Jesus worked with his hands as a carpenter. Paul worked with his hands as a tent maker. God calls us to a life of service, and that requires we use our hands to help others.

Within twenty minutes the teacher had changed his clothes and dropped into a ditch to work with his hands. I do not know what happened to the long fingernail.

We constructed four classrooms for the Free Methodist Church, each about fourteen by twenty feet. They used these rooms for high school students.

The fourth project involved building a parsonage for the Church of the Nazarene. My brother, Floyd, called a few friends to put together a small work team that put up the walls and installed the metal roof on a four-room house. Five college students came to Dessalines to help me install the windows and do interior work.

My work with all of the congregations and pastors in Dessalines created goodwill among the Christians. The four pastors joined together for an outdoor religious meeting in the town square while Floyd was in town. He preached the sermon at that meeting.

I met Francine the summer I went to Dessalines with the Teen Mission team. While the orphanage director was away after the death of his father, Francine worked with me on the dining hall project. One day we needed a board at least ten feet long to use as a screed in finishing the concrete floor. Since we could not find anything straight enough, Francine said he would cut one. We laid a board on sawhorses and used a chalk line to snap a line. The line showed that we needed to trim away about five-eighths of an inch in the middle and taper down to nothing on both ends. Francine grabbed the saw with both hands, teeth away from him, and cut from one end to the other without stopping. I held up the board to inspect the cut. Straight. Perfect. Simply amazing. I smiled at Francine.

When we returned to live at the orphanage for six months, I looked forward to working with Francine again. During our first conversation, Francine told me that he had a good job with a contractor building a large school. They paid him $4.00 per day; the standard wage for a skilled worker was

$1.70 per day. So I simply told my friend of my joy that he had a good job.

Francine came to visit me the next morning. He told me that he did not sleep well the night before. In the morning he went to the school and quit his good job. "I want to work for you because you're my Christian brother," he told me. We had great fellowship for the next six months. Francine was indeed my Christian brother. Francine became my teacher. He helped me learn about the Haitian culture and how I could better function in an environment that often seemed strange to me. I gradually learned to speak Creole.

Francine and his family were active in the Free Methodist Church. His pastor told me that he never initiated any change in the congregation without seeking counsel from Francine. Francine was a soft-spoken man, but he had become one of the strongest leaders in the congregation of three hundred fifty members. I asked the pastor how a young man, just thirty-three years old at the time, developed such wisdom and spiritual maturity. The pastor answered my question with a story.

"Last school year," he began, "I hired Francine's mother to be the cook for our school. Four hundred fifty children must be fed each day at noon. Since Madame Francine took over the job, no food has been lost or stolen. She keeps the cornmeal, beans, rice, and powdered milk under her bed. Even when she is hungry or when her family members need something to eat, she will not take anything." The pastor punctuated his story with one more sentence: "Madame Francine is completely converted."

With that story I knew how Francine developed his strong character. His mother lived such a holy life that her children learned the way of God.

On one of our trips returning to Dessalines from Port-au-Prince, along the highway I saw a man holding a large red snapper, nearly three feet long and maybe twenty-five pounds.

I stopped and purchased the fish for seven dollars. The price was a bargain for me, but for Francine it equaled wages for three and a half days. Once back at the orphanage, I showed the fish to Francine and he agreed to clean it for us. I watched as Francine sat on a concrete block and held the fish to the concrete floor with his bare feet. He used a machete to rake the big scales off of the fish. I suggested that we cook the fish so we could more easily peel off the skin. Francine said that he wanted to eat the skin, so he continued working.

The next morning, Francine walked through the front gate like an old crippled man. He sat down and showed me the bottom of his feet. Rats had smelled the fish and eaten the bottom of his feet in the night. I could see the teeth marks. It looked like someone had scraped a warm candle with the tines of a dinner fork.

I asked why he did not wake up. He told me that when a rat blows on your skin, the skin goes to sleep and you do not feel anything until you wake up. I did not believe him. I think my friend just worked so hard during the day that as he lay on a grass mat at night he slept soundly.

We had two empty five-gallon paint cans after one job. These were buckets with lids, covered with chocolate brown enamel paint. Without thinking much about it, I asked Francine if he wanted the buckets. "I have never had a friend like you," he said. I did not expect that kind of response. He went on to explain that even if he puts his food in a sack and hangs it from the rafters of his house, the rats find a way to get to it. With these buckets, once he had all of the paint scraped off, he could put his food in the metal can, close it with the metal lid, put a rock on the lid, and keep the rats away from the food he needed to provide for his wife and three children. I never knew a bucket could be so important.

Before we left Dessalines at the end of the six months, I helped Francine pour a concrete floor in his mother's house.

On land adjacent to his mother's place, Francine had the walls of his own four-room house up to the bottom of the windows when we returned to the United States. I was glad to help my Christian brother.

Near to the end of our time working together, I put together a collection of tools Francine could use in his own construction projects: a wheelbarrow, shovels, picks, ladder, four-foot level, hammers, chisels, hack saw and blades, and on and on. Some of the tools were brand new; others were the tools we had been using for six months.

I could almost see a light come on in Francine's brain with this gift. A carpenter without tools is a laborer. A carpenter with tools is a contractor. Because everyone in Dessalines saw us together, and since they knew I could be trusted, they trusted Francine. After 1979, Francine worked as a self-employed building contractor.

The blue Chevrolet Suburban we drove throughout that summer had starter issues. Every time we needed to start the vehicle, I placed a piece of cardboard under the car, lay down, and slid to the back of the motor where the starter was mounted (or was supposed to be mounted—the starter hung at a weird angle). I used two pick handles to move the starter into position, one to lift the starter to the correct level and the other to push the starter forward so that the gears engaged with the flywheel. Once I had everything in place, I yelled for Karen to turn the key. It worked . . . until the aluminum casing broke completely. The power steering pump went out about the same time. Unfortunately (or maybe fortunately, read the next paragraph), this happened in Port-au-Prince. Staff members would have to run the orphanage while we waited for the car to be repaired.

Missionary Flights International (MFI) supports missionaries throughout the Caribbean region. We contacted the office in Florida, they purchased the parts we needed, and put them on the next plane to Port-au-Prince. Because this took several days, the four of us spent almost a week in Port-au-Prince waiting for the parts. We stayed at a guest house that cost fifteen dollars per night.

One evening we decided to be adventurous. We hailed a taxi and asked the driver to take us to a restaurant good for white people (as the Haitians called us). "Which one?" he asked. We told him that we were visitors to Port-au-Prince and asked him to select the restaurant for us. When we walked inside, we saw linen tablecloths. Beverage glasses had ice in them. The restaurant had a salad bar. Ceiling fans kept us cool. The staff provided wonderful table service.

Part way through the meal, Shela said, "If we can eat in places like this sometimes, I don't care if we live in Haiti."

That evening back at the guest house, Karen and I had time for a private conversation as we lay on our army cots. We began to look for appropriate ways we could balance our lives of service with self-care for our girls and ourselves. We decided to travel from Dessalines to Port-au-Prince every other week on a Saturday. On Sunday we would attend an English-speaking church service. We would do our shopping on Monday and drive back to Dessalines on Tuesday after meeting the MFI airplane. After making the trip a few times, we began stopping for a swim in the beautiful Caribbean partway back to the orphanage. Karen and I rejoiced when we recognized that our daughters willingly joined us in the mission.

Near the end of our six months in Dessalines, one day a couple with their four-year-old daughter surprised us with a visit. They had heard of us and drove to Dessalines to meet us. After introductions, we sat in the living room with cold sodas. Their little girl went outside to play with the orphans.

The man asked us about how we were adjusting to life in Haiti. At that very moment, before I could respond, the four-year-old burst through the door and made an announcement. "Those white girls have taken off their clothes and are taking a bath with those black people." The man stumbled over how to respond to his daughter, but finally blurted out that it seemed we had adapted well to life in Haiti.

The man did not know the whole story. The corn in our garden grew more than seven feet high. A pitcher pump sat in the middle of the cornfield. The orphan girls flipped their dresses over their heads, got on their hands and knees under the spigot, and let a friend pump water over their backs. Then they stood and flipped their dresses so they hung on their shoulders. This provided an easy way to cool off on a hot afternoon. Karen and I did not know that Shela and Sher'ri cooled off this way too.

Watching our daughters easily adapt to a culture very different from what they knew in Oregon contributed to our growing willingness to consider new options presented to us. We increasingly became aware of opportunities that required serious consideration. We also felt deep within our spirits the strong inclination to go as a call came to us for assistance.

Chapter 4

Be Patient in Suffering

True courage is knowing how to suffer.

~ Haitian Proverb

We decided to move to Haiti. We knew the skills we brought with us could fill the gap for many mission agencies. We put the house we built on the market. That had been a dream house, but our dreams had changed. We purchased another house and converted it to a duplex. We intended to support ourselves with the income from this property. We started collecting everything we would need to live and work in Haiti.

When I became too busy with the preparations to continue working at the construction company, I went to the office to pick up my final paycheck. My boss invited me into his office and told me to close the door. In my seven years of working with him, this was the only time I saw his office door closed. My boss began the conversation by thanking me for my faithfulness and integrity as an employee. Then he became very serious. He told me that he did not approve of Karen and me taking our children to Haiti. He also had two daughters; many times our two families had been together. My boss went on to

50

say, "The world needs people like you, but I do not want it to be you." This was clearly an emotional moment, a side of my boss that I had never seen before. Toward the end of the conversation, my boss held both of my hands and said, "We're going to miss you, boy." He repeated those words over and over; "We're going to miss you, boy."

This man had been my mentor. We often worked together. He taught me to think in creative ways since every major renovation job uncovered something that could not be anticipated. He always inspected my work and I liked it when he approved of what I had done. Later I thought of him and the joy I would experience if he visited me in Haiti to inspect a job.

I said goodbye and opened the door. As I walked through the office I said goodbye to the secretary. Tears came easily as I drove away.

As we worked our way through the to-do list, we decided we could be ready to leave Oregon on July 5. We would join the festivities with our friends at the annual Fourth of July picnic, then start the drive across the United States.

The rental house we purchased needed a lot of repairs. In the rehab process, we converted it into an up-and-down duplex. On July 1, I just needed to install an outdoor light high on the flagpole to complete the remodeling work. My father and a teenage boy I often hired worked with me that day. I set steel scaffolding beside the pole and put a sheet of plywood on top as a platform. Since the scaffolding did not quite reach where I intended to hang the yard light, I put a stepladder on top of the platform.

My father had been watching me. "That looks dangerous," my father said.

"I'll be okay," I responded. The ladder stood far enough from the edge of the platform to be safe.

He still insisted that we do something to secure the ladder. He threw a rope to me so I could tie everything together.

The rope landed behind me. As I stepped back to grab the end of the rope, the plywood tilted up and I went over backwards with the plywood. I fell seventeen feet to the concrete driveway.

I hit the concrete in a sitting position with my right hand, my heels, and my tailbone hitting the pavement at the same time. I tried to get up. My right hand hung like a sock full of sand. I used my left hand to stabilize my right arm. After a call to 911, a trip to the hospital, and a thorough examination in the emergency room, the doctor gave me the bad news. I had broken my left leg and heel and two places in my lower back. My right hand and wrist had shattered, somewhere between thirty and fifty fractures.

I watched carefully as the doctor positioned a drill bit on the back of my right hand. He drilled through the skin and bone and left about one inch of a stainless steel pin sticking out. He put another pin in my elbow leaving the end exposed also. He put my fingers and thumb into a holder suspended from the ceiling and hung a twenty-five-pound sandbag below my bicep. This contraption stretched my arm to the proper length. The doctor began to twist and push on my wrist, molding it back into the right shape. He adjusted the bones in my arm and wrist six times or more. Finally he said, "This looks really good." I took him at his word since it looked awful to me. Then the doctor put a plaster cast on my right arm to keep everything from shifting in the weeks ahead. He put my left leg in a cast too. My left arm was not injured, so that is where they stuck the IV.

Since I anticipated leaving on July 5, in the middle of June I had written to the health insurance company to cancel our policy. Karen called the company immediately. If we had let the policy lapse by not paying the premium, we could have reinstated it. Because we had canceled the policy, I lay in the hospital bed with no medical insurance.

About this time the man who purchased our house called to inform me that he was backing out of the deal. I explained to the man that the contract did not have contingencies, that his reason for nixing the agreement was outside of the legal parameters. I explained my predicament, my accident, and my need for the funds from the sale of the house to apply to the purchase of the rental property. He told me that he just needed to do what he needed to do and hung up the telephone. I contacted an attorney to begin proceedings for breach of contract, but I dropped those two weeks later. I had no desire to go through another drawn-out lawsuit.

As I lay in the hospital bed, alone in the room, I knew I would not be leaving for Haiti on July 5. The doctor told me that we would wait until my arm healed and then do surgery to take out the bones causing the most pain. This was not good news for a right-handed man who makes his living with his hands. I had intended to be a helper in Haiti; instead I was handicapped. I wanted to be a hero; now I depended totally on the heroic efforts of others.

My financial woes compounded the severe physical injuries. I faced hospital bills with no health insurance. I had no income. The sale of our dream house fell through, so now we had two houses to finance. Our household belongings had been packed, but we obviously would not be going anywhere soon. The accident seemed to prompt some friends to bring up their concern for our daughters' well-being while living in an impoverished country like Haiti. With all these things working against me, it seemed like I clung tightly to a tree as high winds and heavy rains pounded me.

Visitors started coming to the hospital. Nearly everyone assumed I would not move to Haiti. The prosperity movement in the evangelical church had influenced some of my friends, so they saw my suffering as a sign of God's displeasure. I have to admit, a comparison of my situation and their model seemed made for each other as the example to be avoided. In their thinking, my next steps logically lay before me.

One friend asked me, "Well, what is God trying to tell you through all this?"

I looked at him in disbelief. I responded with a raised voice in total frustration. "What is God trying to teach me? Nothing! Not one thing! God does not communicate with me by pushing me off of a seventeen-foot platform and dropping me on concrete."

God had my attention before I fell off of the scaffolding. I had already discovered how God's mission permeated the Bible from beginning to end. I heard God's direction in the sermon text of a Haitian student preacher. Is the Great Commission only for Christians who are healthy, well-funded, and without children? Is the gospel good news for all persons in all cultural contexts in all circumstances? Did Jesus come for the whole world or only healthy, wealthy Americans? The implications of what my friends said aggravated me. I had listened to the cassette tapes of the preachers they liked. I stopped tapes to look up the Bible references the preachers mentioned and saw how time after time the passage had been crammed into an idea contrary to the Christian scriptures. I had read the Bible and knew it had nothing to do with getting my share of the blessing, but joining God on the mission.

Now, I believe that God heals broken bodies. But Jesus does not hurt someone just to have the opportunity to do a miracle. Besides, I have no desire to serve a God who beats up a person as a show of power and might. And it makes no sense to follow God just to make the suffering stop. That type of coercion pushes persons away from God; it does not pull them toward the God of grace, mercy, and love described in the Bible.

So what was God trying to teach me? Not a thing! My friend looked stunned at my response. "As soon as I can walk," I continued, "I'm moving to Haiti!"

Through everything that happened, I kept looking for the open door. My friends, in contrast, seemed more interested in finding a closed door. Others tried to divert my attention away from God's mission. My physical pain and my financial crisis loomed large before me. I could have easily shifted my focus. Instead, somehow, my determination to go to Haiti strengthened even as I lay in the hospital bed.

But I felt alone on the journey. My friends remained cordial, but they failed to understand my convictions and priorities. They wanted my family and me to be comfortable and secure. I talked to Karen about the days ahead and we agreed to continue moving toward the way that opened before us, confident that God led the way.

I could not get out of bed. I could not even get myself on a bedpan. A male nurse, a large, strong man, scooped me in his arms and held me while I used the bedpan. It felt so good to be held by that man.

I wanted to get out of the hospital as soon as possible, but first I needed to get past the physical therapist. I hurt all over. My left heel was broken, but my right heel hurt even worse. Because my right hand was totally out of commission, I was given a special crutch to use on the right side. Once the IVs were out of my left arm I could use a standard crutch on the left side. I needed crutches because my left leg was in a cast. My lower back was supported by a body brace. To satisfy the physical therapy requirements, I had to walk up three steps and down three steps before they would release me. I found those three steps to be nearly impossible to negotiate. After multiple attempts and almost as many failures, they let me go home.

But I had no home. All of our household items had been moved to storage. So we stayed with my brother, Floyd, as we tried to figure out the next steps. We received assistance from the government to help us pay the medical bills and give us funds for living expenses. We sold the duplex, but just broke even after all of our remodeling. We found a renter for the dream house.

About forty days after my accident, we put our green Land Cruiser inside a moving truck. I figured that since I could not work, I might as well sit in a truck rather than just sit at my brother's house. Behind the truck we towed a small cargo trailer full of tools and personal items. Karen drove the truck. The girls sat in the middle. I sat in the passenger seat. I still wore the back brace, a boot on my left leg, and the original cast on my right arm, so sometimes sitting in the truck seat was very uncomfortable. Traveling from Oregon to Florida in August in a truck with no air conditioning made for difficult conditions. We felt uncomfortable, but at least we headed in the right direction.

When we arrived in Birmingham, Alabama, I looked through the telephone book and found an orthopedic surgeon to look at my arm. He took an x-ray and then removed the cast I had lugged around for several weeks. At first he tried to pull the pin from the back of my hand with a special tool, but the pliers slipped off of the pin. It hurt . . . bad. The doctor apologized and asked the nurse to get "old faithful." The nurse opened the cabinet doors under the sink and retrieved a pair of vice grips. I suddenly liked this doctor a lot more. He adjusted the vice grips and snapped it on the pin. He twisted back and forth a couple times, then pulled the pin out. The vice grips did the trick with the pin in the elbow too.

As the surgeon looked at my arm, he said, "Whoever set this arm did a wonderful job." I appreciated the good news. The doctor put a second cast on my arm that came nearly to my elbow. We paid the doctor in cash and he sent us on our way with the hope that perhaps I would never need surgery to take out some of the bone fragments in my hand.

I removed the second cast myself in Haiti by using a pair of tin snips. I had x-rays and saw an orthopedic surgeon visiting Haiti. He said words almost identical to what I heard from the doctor in Birmingham; my original doctor had done a great job. This orthopedist told me I could begin physical therapy. "PT will hurt," he said, "but remember, no pain, no gain."

I found an American physical therapist in Haiti. As we got started, she asked, "How much flexibility would you like to have with this arm?" I told her that I wanted to use the arm: to swing a hammer, throw a baseball, and pickup and use a skill saw with one hand.

Her reply shocked me. "You are going to suffer," she said. "The degree to which your flexibility returns will be in direct correlation to the pain you tolerate." I began to push myself to endure more and more pain. While sitting in church I put the palm of my hand on the seat beside me and pushed down. I would hold it . . . hold it . . . hold it . . . until the pain burned like fire in my wrist. Then I slipped my right hand in my left armpit and crossed my arms over my chest. I sat that way listening to the sermon until the pain subsided. I learned to do all kinds of things while driving the car that flexed my right wrist. When I first began to use a hammer, each swing brought pain. Each pull on a wrench, each twist on a screwdriver handle, each pain in my wrist signaled that I needed to continue physical therapy. It took a full year before I felt like my right arm was not disabled.

For the first few months in Haiti, I had only one pair of shoes that felt good on my feet. I could barely walk barefoot. Getting out of bed in the morning, I found it necessary to hang on to furniture as I made my way towards the bathroom. Touching my heels to the floor caused pain to shoot up my legs.

My suffering caused me to slow down, to take my foot off life's accelerator. I had time to stop and look and listen. I had always been proud of my strong body. I often told Karen that I could work twenty-four hours a day if my legs would not get tired. I loved to work. After the accident, in my first few months in Haiti, I constantly looked for a place to sit down. I often needed to lie on the sofa for a mid-afternoon nap.

Prior to this accident, I often thought of sick people as wimpy. This accident changed that opinion. In a sense, the physical therapist's prediction that full restoration of my right hand and arm would only come through pain creates an image true in other ways. As I look back, I remember story after story where I found that the greater the sacrifice or suffering, the greater the joy. I did not want to be someone who worked hard to avoid uncomfortable situations, to intentionally dodge risk and look for the most secure way to live. "Be patient in suffering," Paul told the Christians in Rome (Rom. 12:12). Because of the suffering I endured, I found that I had much more empathy with those who suffer. The discipline of suffering opened doors for some of my most meaningful experiences. I do not understand why people go to such great lengths and expense to avoid suffering when at the other end something redemptive occurs.

We took the Land Cruiser out of the moving truck in Fort Lauderdale. We moved the vehicle and trailer to the docks to be shipped to Haiti. About two weeks after flying to Haiti, we received news that the vehicle and trailer had arrived. But we had a big problem. In those days, Haiti had a regulation that a vehicle could not be brought into the country if it was more than three years old. Our Land Cruiser was about ten years old.

"What can I do now?" I asked the customs officer. "The vehicle is already here."

"Dump it in the ocean," he replied. "You cannot drive that vehicle in this country." End of conversation.

On several occasions I talked with the freight forwarder helping us to clear customs. I always heard the same message: I could take my trailer, but not the Land Cruiser.

After three weeks of frustration, I received a telephone call saying that our personal items were ready for release from customs. To our great surprise, someone changed the date on the title to the Land Cruiser. According to the official document, we now owned a nearly new vehicle. I did not ask questions. Later I called the freight forwarder to ask if she had paid a bribe. She had not, but thought I did. Nope.

We still needed to have the Land Cruiser and trailer inspected. I had secured the cargo trailer's back door with about seventy-five screws. I did not have a power drill in those days, so I did it all by hand. I limped across the hot parking lot, a cast on my right arm, a Phillips screwdriver in my left hand. The inspector did not hide his frustration with me as I struggled to remove seventy-five screws.

When I finally opened the trailer door, we discovered a big mess. The last package to go into the trailer was a box of jam that Karen's mother had made for us. She had used paraffin wax to seal the jars. By accident the box was put into the trailer upside down. The wax melted as we traveled across the United States and as the trailer sat on the hot docks in Florida and Haiti. The jam ran from the top to the bottom and covered everything in the back of the trailer.

In shaky English, the inspector said, "What the hell is this?"

In my best Creole, I answered, "Food."

"Why did you do this?"

"It was an accident."

"Close the door," he told me. "Take this and leave."

So I did. We washed everything with a garden hose as we unloaded the trailer.

We eagerly got our house organized because we were tired of living out of suitcases.

Chapter 5

No-name Street

Little by little the bird builds a nest.
~ Haitian Proverb

I love to watch people so I can peek into their day-to-day lives and hopefully become more comfortable in their culture. In the early 1980s, a no-name street in downtown Port-au-Prince, Haiti, became my classroom as I sat in the shadows to avoid the Caribbean sun. It was the first street off of the main highway. I sat near a power pole, about sixty feet from an intersection. I had just enough room to park my motorcycle. Then I sat and watched.

I found this spot because that is where I went to use the unofficial Haitian post office. When the starter went out on our car, for example, we did not have telephone service to let the orphanage staff know that our return would be delayed. But we did have a private mail service. About a half-dozen trucks made the round trip between Dessalines and Port-au-Prince every day but Sunday. These trucks offloaded on the no-name street in Port-au-Prince. I would be there when the truck rumbled in. I paid someone catching a ride back to Dessalines to hand deliver my letter to the orphanage staff. When the truck came rolling down the dusty road in Dessalines about six in the evening, the messenger walked to the orphanage to deliver the letter. I probably used this mail service a dozen times and my private mail carrier always came through.

As I waited for a big truck to arrive on the no-name street, I sat in the shadows and watched and listened. I tried to blend into the landscape so I could learn to love people very different from me.

I once took a friend from the United States with me to my hide-a-way classroom. That day we watched men unloading one hundred pound sacks of corn. Men inside the open-roofed truck rolled the heavy sacks onto the backs of men standing on the ground. Off they went in a hurry and disappeared into a one-story warehouse. These men dripped with sweat as they worked as fast as possible. The team received a fixed amount of compensation once they completed the job.

I told my friend to look at the old woman across the street. At first he saw only the busyness all around us—passing cars, food vendors pushing carts, people walking by. "Look under the truck," I said. Then he saw her, a small woman sitting under the truck, holding a tin can, the size soup comes in, and picking up one piece of corn at a time as it fell through the floor of the truck. The truck provided shade so she could avoid the hot noonday sun as she diligently waited for another kernel to fall.

On another day when I needed to send a letter to Dessalines, I sat on my motorcycle while I waited. I made eye contact with a streetwise boy about ten years old. He greeted me warmly, and then said in perfect English, "Give me fifty thousand dollars!"

Game on! In a gruff voice I responded in Creole, "For what?"

Our eyes locked onto each other. This time he spoke in Creole and, in hushed tones, asked if I could feed him. He said he was very hungry.

Just up the street to my left, a woman sold bowls of cooked rice and beans. I bought him a man-sized bowl. He stood near me and ate with the soupspoon the woman provided. He ate every bean, every grain of rice.

After he ate, my shirtless friend remained near me. We never touched, but he stayed close. Perhaps ten minutes after he finished eating, my little buddy made another request. He asked for "tiny money."

Again, I played the role of the tough guy. "For what?" I growled.

"I'm thirsty," came his quiet reply.

A woman with water on her head stood nearby. She sold about twenty ounces of water for five cents. She poured water into the one glass she carried and handed it to the boy. He tipped up the glass and drank all the water in one continuous gulp. I let the boy keep the change from the twenty cents I gave him for the water. He could have "tiny money" in his pocket for a while.

I kept watching this boy as he blended into the sights and sounds and smells of the multitude moving up and down a no-name street. In my mind I still see a vivid picture of a skinny, shirtless, barefoot boy with an extended stomach clearly full of food and water. I remember the final goodbye when this boy gave me a slight smile and quickly lifted his eyebrows. I knew he had enough to eat for that day, but the next he would have to hustle again in order to survive. As I sat on my motorcycle, I figured things worked out well for me. The boy initially demanded fifty thousand dollars. In the end, it only cost me about sixty cents.

About noon one day I found myself stuck in an alley trying to get onto a busy, four-lane road. Just about the time a break in the traffic came, a pedestrian walked in front of my car and I would have to linger longer. As I waited, I reached into my lunch bag and began to eat. Two street vendors sat on short wooden stools about ten feet from me, one selling cookies and chewing gum and the other selling fruit from an open basket. People had tossed garbage in a pile behind the women. A man in a suit, about forty years old, stood next to the garbage holding a baseball cap in his left hand. I saw him bend over to pick up rotting banana peels that he put in the cap. He used the fingers of one hand to roll a little ball out of the peels before he popped it in his mouth; no chewing, just swallowed.

Through an open window, I called this Haitian fellow to come talk with me. He quickly responded. We looked eye to eye as he stood beside my vehicle with his baseball cap held behind him. I greeted him in Creole and asked how he was doing. "I'm doing well," he said, "thanks for asking." I am not sure what I said next, but I clearly remember his reply: "I'm cooking with gas!" That means he was eating, not food cooked on an open fire or even using charcoal, but he cooked his food on a gas stove.

I did not know how to respond. I had watched him eat three balls of blackened banana peels taken off of a trash pile. Finally, I called him my friend and told him what I had observed. His head dropped and he told me that he was very hungry. I handed him a brown paper bag with clean food inside, added some money, and wished him well. I saw a break in the traffic and sped away.

As I drove up the mountain, I kept wondering if I had given enough. Questions like that still trouble me.

One afternoon in 1981, a friend gave me a ride into Port-au-Prince. I intended to catch a _tap tap_ on no-name street to get back up the mountain to our house. A _tap tap_ is a shared taxi service in Haiti. Riders climb into the back of a small pickup truck and sit on benches running front to back on each side. The benches are close enough that the knees of riders facing each other often touch. The seats

63

have backrests, so the open air ride is not only cheap, but fairly comfortable. When the truck comes near your destination, you rap on the fender, jump out, and pay the driver.

On this day it seemed like all of the *tap taps* were maxed out. The five o'clock rush hour was on and people scrunched together like hot dogs still in the wrapper. I resigned myself to getting home later than I expected.

One *tap tap* driver saw me and stopped. I looked at the full pickup truck. Not one person made eye contact with me. So I waved the driver on.

"Get in," he yelled.

"You're full," I shouted back as I waved him on again.

"Get in!" he insisted.

I walked to the back of the truck. All dozen of the people in the *tap tap* stared at each other, not at me. From about six feet back, I ran forward and dove onto their laps, my arms outstretched. I had just performed the greatest belly flop of my life. Silence lingered just a split second, then the people in the back of that pickup exploded with laughter.

I still lay sprawled on their laps when the driver started moving. Somehow they made room for me to wiggle onto the bench. Then everyone wanted to talk to me. Where do you live? How long have you been in Haiti? Do you like Haiti?

Many Haitians live in difficult circumstances. Life is hard. They work long hours for little compensation. They sleep on grass mats on the ground. On that day, about five in the afternoon, a crazy American gave a bunch of people a reason to laugh. I hope it refreshed them as much as it did me.

One day in December, Shela joined me on no-name street. She was fourteen years old at the time. We sat quietly as we waited for a friend, watching the people rush by.

Off to the side we noticed a woman, about my age, taking a bath in a pothole in the street. The hole held perhaps a gallon of water, a free gift from a slow leak in a buried waterline.

64

She sang as she bathed. Shela and I glanced at the woman from time to time, watching as she cupped her hands again and again to get some water. A truck sat parked a few steps away from the pothole. The woman continued singing as she combed her hair while looking in the truck's side mirror. Her last handful of water went into her mouth as she brushed her teeth with an index finger.

One of the strange things about December in Haiti was the music. Everywhere we went, through loudspeakers we heard the clear, mellow voice of Bing Crosby singing, "I'm dreaming of a White Christmas." Very few Haitians spoke English, so why was this woman singing along with an American icon?

Haiti was hot and dry in December. White dust hung like fog around our rented house. The dirt and gravel road in front of our house became the primary reason why our family sang "White Christmas." Two sides of our home had no window glass; there were only open security bars. The white dust off of the road drifted into our three-bedroom home, a dust as fine as cornstarch. Noel, our family cat, left white footprints on the coffee-colored dining room table every night. When our Christmas celebrations ended, we carried our plastic Christmas tree outside to hose off the dust.

During the years we lived in Haiti, singing "White Christmas" became our favorite family holiday tradition. Year after year, we listened as loudspeakers blasted Bing Crosby's voice over the hot dusty streets. We joined the Haitians as they sang along.

During our last Christmas season in Haiti, a street worker washed a friend's car in downtown Port-au-Prince. As he worked, he sang, "I'm dreaming of a white Christmas." My friend asked the worker a simple question; "Do you understand the words to that song?"

"Oh, yes," the street worker replied.

"When did you see snow?"

"Sir, I don't know snow. I only know the song."

"Well, what does this song mean?"

"I'm dreaming of a white Christmas. You know, a Christmas with food and a bed and gifts to give my family. I'm dreaming of a Christmas like white people have."

I continue to ponder that statement. How did we end up with Christmas being about stuff? In the years since I heard the street worker make that statement, I have been revamping my priorities. Year after year I have humbled myself and submitted to the teachers God has given me. The poor have become my heroes. They show me hope! Saints who suffer, sing, and smile, well, they influence me. Those who are poor in spirit hold the secrets for happiness and I must somehow look beyond their gender, age, race, education, and economic status. It started in 1980 when God used a woman on a no-name street to begin teaching me that a dream and a song for Christmas may not seem like much where I came from, but it's essential.

Chapter 6

Walking Home Together

An empty sack cannot stand up.
~ Haitian Proverb

I n the middle of the night in 1983, a violent tropical storm
hit La Gonâve, an island eleven miles out in the ocean from
Port-au-Prince. Accompanied by very heavy rains, the wind
lifted the roof trusses off of the only hospital on the island.
The La Gonâve Wesleyan Hospital staff, working frantically in
the darkness, moved patients to safety, or at least into an area
of the building that still provided some shelter from the wind
and rain.

As the chaos subsided, hospital staff realized that they had
lost track of one patient. A man about forty years old came to
the hospital because he had broken his back. The doctor put him
in traction to aid his healing. He had a boot around each foot
and ankle. The boots had ropes attached that went through a
pulley to a sandbag. Because the pulleys were anchored to the
roof structure, when the roof blew off it took the man with it.
The poor man could not yell for help because of his shock. He
survived the ordeal and remained in the hospital at the time I
made my first visit to the island.

As soon as they could, the hospital staff put out an urgent call for help. They decided to install a concrete roof over the hospital to better withstand future storms. I signed on to manage the project.

To make such a large pour, I took a concrete mixer on the eleven-mile journey to the island. We used a boat about seven feet wide and twenty-four feet long. It had a canvas sail and a twenty-five horsepower motor. We placed two heavy planks across the width of the boat, and situated the mixer on the planks. We used ropes and come-along cables to secure the five-hundred-pound mixer. The boat captain liked the way things looked when we stepped back to assess our work.

All went well on our trip from Port-au-Prince to the island. The trip back several weeks later was a different story.

We already had the mixer loaded for the return trip when the winds started blowing. The captain wanted to delay until the following day. I disagreed. Since we had the mixer loaded, I said, "Let's go." The captain surrendered to my insistence and off we went.

About halfway through what typically was a two-hour trip, we encountered huge waves. The captain worked like crazy to keep the nose of the boat going into the waves. If a wave caught the side of the boat, we would surely flip because of the way we had situated the concrete mixer. I watched as over and over the ends of the planks dipped into the water as the boat rocked. I could see that it would not take much for us to capsize. We were in big trouble.

The boat had a hand pump for clearing water from the boat. The captain's helper put his foot on the pump and pulled the handle up and down to discharge water from inside the boat. He did this for more than an hour without stopping. I had a friend with me on this trip and we frantically retightened the ropes and cables that held our concrete mixer. Many times I thought we had lost the battle in the middle of the ocean.

When we approached the dock, the boat still bounced like a cork bobbing on the water. As we came alongside the wooden dock, the end of one of the planks came up under the dock and flipped part of the dock six feet in the air. Even as the ocean continued to surge and the boat continued to rock, we found a way to push the mixer off of the boat onto what remained of the dock. We eventually moved the mixer onto dry ground. What a relief.

The captain's helper showed me his hand. He had large blisters from pumping.

I apologized to the captain. I had no business pushing this man to do something he recognized as dangerous. It pleased me that I did not lose the mixer valued at over three thousand dollars, but it would have been devastating if someone had died because of my foolhardiness. My willingness to take risk put others in jeopardy. Over the next few years, I used the same boat many times to haul building materials to La Gonâve, but I never again told the captain how to do his job.

La Gonâve island is thirty-seven miles long and nine miles wide. The highest point on the island reaches 2,552 feet above the beautiful blue Caribbean. Because of the steep limestone mountainsides, very few roads exist on the island. This requires friends to carry people who need medical assistance to the hospital. Sometimes they used a straight-back chair strapped to two poles to transport the sick person, often walking for miles. People on the side of the island away from the hospital could travel faster by boat.

I learned that over the years more than one hundred thousand different people had been treated at the La Gonâve Wesleyan Hospital. The meticulous hospital filing system consisted of three-by-five-inch index cards with hand-written notes that identified the patients by name and village location.

The hospital roof project posed quite a few challenges, heavy and dangerous. We took off the old roof structure. We built the forms for the new concrete roof, then installed electrical conduit. It took forty-five minutes round trip with an old rusty car to pull a trailer to the sandpit, shovel sand onto the trailer, drive back to the hospital, and offload the sand near the concrete mixer. Once the workers finished a batch of concrete, we carried it in buckets up ladders to pour the roof. The work proved to be tedious in the hot Caribbean sun.

I constructed a new surgical room at the La Gonâve Wesleyan Hospital, about eighteen by twenty feet. This had a concrete roof and tile floor. A heavy, old lamp hung from the ceiling above the surgical table that worked only when the hospital ran a generator. I built and installed base and upper cabinets on three walls to hold surgical supplies that had to be shipped to the island. They used a large pressure cooker to sterilize the surgical instruments. The pressure cooker sat over a charcoal fire just outside of the operation room. When the weight on top of the pressure valve began to wiggle and rattle, someone moved the cooker to the concrete sidewalk to cool before returning it to the operating room with the clean instruments inside.

One day the hospital staff invited me to lay aside my tools and watch the surgeries. I accepted the invitation with a great deal of anticipation.

One operation I watched involved a woman in her mid-twenties, petite, no more than five feet two inches tall and one hundred pounds. She had a pleasant face and buoyant disposition. She expressed her gratitude to God as the nurses prepared her for surgery. She looked nine months pregnant, but the doctor knew it was a tumor that had been growing for many years.

The surgery went quickly. I left the room when the doctor finished. When a nurse came by carrying the tumor in a light blue plastic basin, I followed her into a side room. The nurse put the tumor on the scale; it weighed exactly ten pounds. The nurse returned to the operating room and I heard her tell the others the weight. While some of the nurses started getting ready for the next operation, I watched the doctor use a scalpel to open the tumor like a cook would open a melon. He held the two pieces apart for just a moment, but long enough for me to see healthy flesh, black hair, and white adult teeth. I do not recall any words spoken at that time. Later one of the medical personnel told me that this growth likely had been the woman's twin growing inside of her since birth (*fetus in fetu*).

I have observed other surgeries and medical procedures in mission hospitals. The missionary doctors deal with a variety of medical emergencies and health issues, just as hospitals do in the United States. The distinction, however, is that the doctors in mission areas work in modest buildings with basic equipment. Sometimes they have to do exploratory surgery simply because they do not have diagnostic equipment for x-rays and scans. Somehow they make do with what they have and lovingly care for those who otherwise suffered needlessly. I eagerly used my construction skills to make things a bit easier for the dedicated medical staff.

During our trips to the island, I became friends with a sixteen-year-old boy dying of cancer. My friend, David, wore a baseball-style cap with a California State Police logo. He slept in a room just big enough for a single bed. The missionary staff fed him. David's cancer was in his nose; one of the American nurses regularly went to his room to change the bandage.

David liked to stay close to me, but the smell created a big problem. I learned to love this boy, but sometimes without warning I would start to gag. I did not like to do that, not at all, but I could not control the reflexive response to the smell.

71

So I learned to make do with short visits. I took a big breath of air, then moved closer to David until my air was gone. I turned away to take another big breath so I could continue the conversation. Sometimes I gave him a hug or teased him by taking his beloved cap and putting it on my own head.

One night I attended a service at the Wesleyan church. I sat about twenty feet from a window. At one point in the service I smelled my friend, David. I look towards the side window and there he was, waiting for me to get out of church so we could walk home together. David was small for his age. I suspect he had cancer for many years. Always polite, David never pushed himself on me, but he was never far away, just waiting for my attention. If I could do it over, I would spend more time with David. I hope someone sat with him when he died.

I met a man named Éclair, in his early twenties, with painful elephantiasis on his right leg just below the knee. His leg had grown to the size of a gallon milk jug. He arrived at the hospital with one hundred dollars to pay for the surgery.

I quietly watched as the surgeons amputated Éclair's leg. The short nurses stood on concrete blocks to reach across the surgical table. The missionary doctor told me that he had never performed this particular procedure. An open textbook lay nearby for reference. I marveled at the skill and care these medical workers provided.

As I observed surgeries in various hospitals, I realized that many physical differences are only skin deep. A surgeon can operate on anyone regardless of race. On another occasion, I donated blood just before the cancer surgery of a pastor's wife in Haiti. A bag of my warm blood lay on her stomach as they wheeled her into the operating room. Blood is just blood, a river of life. After the surgery, this woman told me that she hoped she could learn English more quickly after having my blood in her body. Experiences like this caused me to build solidarity with people unlike me only on the surface.

On the second day after Éclair's surgery, I worked on an exterior door at the hospital. I was surprised to see Éclair using crutches to go to the pit latrines near the back wall of the hospital compound. Coming back to the hospital building, Éclair collapsed about six feet from where I worked. I picked him up and carried him to his hospital bed.

Éclair broke open the incision. Blood and fluids came out. The nurse who responded was obviously frustrated that he walked outside without assistance. With the bandage off, Éclair wanted to see his leg. When he tried to sit up, the nurse put her hand on his chest and shoved him back on the bed. When the nurse left the room to get supplies, I noticed a small mirror on the wall. I quickly took the mirror and held it at the correct angle so Éclair could see his leg. I watched a slight smile form on his face. When I heard the nurse's footsteps, I hurriedly hung the mirror on the wall before she returned. We did not say anything while the nurse re-bandaged his leg. When she left, Éclair said to me, "I know you are my friend."

Over the next few days I stopped by to see Éclair several times. On my last visit, just before I got on the boat to go back to Port-au-Prince, Éclair said he wanted to talk with me about an important matter. Éclair proposed that he go with me to the United States and that I become his father. I let him finish speaking before I replied.

I gave Éclair several reasons why the idea would not work: "I work days and you would not have anyone at home to talk with; the weather in the United States is very cold; you could watch television, but it would not be in Creole; you would miss your friends and family." He agreed with me on every point.

Then he said, "I knew you would tell me no, but it makes me feel good to have a friend like you that I can ask."

As I sat on the boat headed for Port-au-Prince, I thought about Éclair. I imagined him returning to his village in a few days. In my mind I heard him talking about a good friend he met at the hospital, a man from the United States named Swanee. "We even talked about me going to the United States to live with him," I envisioned Éclair saying, "but we decided that probably it would not be a good idea." I looked back over my shoulder as the island of La Gonâve faded from view and thanked God for my new friends.

Chapter 7

Dégagé

*Never talk about the crocodile if you
have to cross the river again.*
~ Haitian Proverb

The largest crew I ever used on a building project involved seventy-six men. Even with such a large group, it took us twelve hours to complete that day's job.

I supervised the construction of four classrooms at the Quisqueya Christian School in Port-au-Prince, Haiti. On one day we poured the concrete roof on a forty-by-eighty-foot, two-story building. We started the two concrete mixers at seven o'clock in the morning, one at each end of the building. Each mixer had sand, gravel, cement, and water nearby. We positioned ladders at both ends of the building. Each team had thirty buckets. Men stood on the ladders, one man's eyes at the level of another man's feet. The workers held the ladder with their left hand and reached down to get the next bucket of concrete with their right hand. Once the buckets reached the roof level, twenty-three feet from the ground, the worker dumped the concrete into a wheelbarrow and slipped a rope through the bucket handle for the zip line ride back to the ground. Workers pushed the wheelbarrows to the appropriate place on the roof and dumped the load where workers used screeds and trowels to finish the concrete. We rotated the workers every thirty minutes, some filling the concrete mixers, others pushing the wheelbarrows, and some standing on the ladder in bare feet, lifting the twenty pounds of concrete, bucket after bucket after bucket. The sounds of singing and laughing filled the air all day. For twelve hours we never shut off the concrete mixers. We used three hundred bags of cement that day and mixed sixty cubic yards of concrete.

When we started, the two crews on the roof worked about eighty feet apart. As we progressed through the day, the crews moved closer to the middle of the building. When the two groups of workers came together in the center at the end of the day, they started in the back of the building and worked their way to the front. When the last bucket of concrete went on the roof near the middle in the front, concrete at the ends of the building where we started was already hard.

A project of this size comes with the potential for accidents in many forms. We stayed safe that day. We went home tired but with smiles on our faces.

Haitians have a word that I found myself often using: dégagé. This Creole word means, "make do," as in figure out a way to get the job done with whatever you have on hand at the moment. In the United States I would go to the hardware store to buy an item designed to do exactly what I needed to do. I did not have that luxury in Haiti and so I often had to improvise. Dégagé.

I directed the construction of an addition on the Grace Children's Hospital in Port-au-Prince. This building previously served as an embassy. The tuberculosis hospital had no use for the L-shaped outdoor swimming pool, so we constructed a concrete building above it. The new room provided a reception area and we converted the pool area underneath into a cool room to store medicines.

Early in the construction process, we installed plastic conduit for electrical wire. By the time we needed to pull the wire through the conduit, we had finished the plaster and stucco. Since the conduit made five bends, I could not get the steel fish tape through the conduit to draw the wire. When working on one end proved unsuccessful, I started from the other end. For more than an hour I labored in vain. Nothing worked. In frustration, I went home for lunch.

When I returned in the afternoon, the Haitian workers showed me that they had pulled the wire. They finished the task without me. I was amazed and wanted to know their secret. The workers told me that they tied a cotton ball on the end of a small thread. They blew the cotton ball through the conduit, around all of the bends, until it came out the other end of the thirty-five feet of conduit. Once they had one string going the distance, they tied on a larger cord and pulled it through. They repeated the process until the steel fish line lay ready to pull the electrical wire. I tried to force a steel line through the conduit. The Haitians used a puff of air. Dégagé.

Several short-term mission teams worked with me on this project. Once tuberculosis treatment started, the children were no longer contagious, so this was a good place for visitors to provide compassionate care for these children. Most of the kids spent twenty-four hours a day in an enamel-painted metal crib. They were starved for attention. When we walked through the doors, twenty eager hands reached out, the children begging to be picked up, talked to, and hugged.

We often worked in rural areas, not Port-au-Prince, in those years. On one project in rural Haiti, two friends and I stayed at a small hotel at a beautiful location: sandy beach, palm trees. The dining room had four tables. On the first night we asked the owner about the menu. He said they served fish, beef, and chicken. We ordered three chicken dinners. He replied, "Three chicken dinners . . . tomorrow night." We realized that he did not have chicken, so we changed our order to fish. He did not have fish available. Or beef. Before we left the dining room, we put in an order for three chicken dinners and sodas. We went back to our room and ate whatever we had in the ice chest. The next evening we enjoyed our sodas while the hotel owner prepared our chicken dinners. When he served the dinner, we each asked for another soda. He told us that when he went to Jacmel for the food, he only purchased three sodas. If we had dinner at his hotel the next night, he assured us, he would have six sodas. During that trip we ate with him each night, placing our dinner order twenty-four hours in advance.

In October 1983, Karen and I traveled to a rural area to finalize plans to bring a construction team to build a church just before Christmas. A leading family in the congregation offered their four-room house for the team to sleep in while we worked on this project. The house needed some maintenance, so when we returned with the team I included screens for the windows and doors and paint for the walls.

Karen and I both drove vehicles with trailers on this trip. The trailer hitch on Karen's vehicle broke on the way to the village. We stopped, unloaded the trailer, set up the welder, and fixed the trailer hitch on the side of the road. The emergency repairs made us late arriving in the village. The rains started soon after we moved our suitcases, sleeping bags, and food into the house. We used one room for cooking, one room for an eating area, one room for the women to sleep in, and one room for the men. I remember being awakened several times during that night with the rain pounding on the tin roof. I was so thankful we were not sleeping in tents.

Early the next morning, one of our team members said, "There was a baby born outside our room last night."

"What?" I replied. "Are you sure?"

"I heard a newborn baby crying last night," he said.

We soon discovered that he was correct. The family who provided the house for us to sleep in, rather than moving in with a neighbor or a relative, had moved into a chicken house just outside the bedroom window. In the midst of a heavy rainstorm, the woman gave birth in the chicken house.

Our whole team felt terrible. We insisted that the woman move back into her home, but this family flatly refused. We were their guests, they told us, and they wanted to give us their best. We humbly accepted their gracious gift. A mother, father, and four children slept in a chicken house while we occupied their four-room house. Since this occurred just before Christmas, I began to see the birth of Jesus in a different light.

In 1982, I worked on a church building in Ki Lundi, high in the mountains of Haiti. Leaving Jacmel, we followed the ocean to the east, and then drove along a river that we eventually crossed eleven times. When we came to the end of the road, we rode mules for three hours. Sometimes the mules could not negotiate the steep path with us on their backs, so we walked beside the mules. About one hundred fifty people gathered for worship on this mountaintop. Twice a hurricane had blown away their church building and we set out to provide a permanent structure.

The pastor told everyone who came to worship on Sundays to bring a building stone with them. When I first visited the site, my friend and I estimated that they had gathered enough stones to build the foundation and walls. We wondered how we could get the other building materials to such a remote location. The pastor responded in three words, "On our heads." We constructed a twenty-eight-by-fifty-foot church building on that mountaintop. Every piece of lumber, every piece of steel, every one of the one hundred bags of cement came up the mountain with someone carrying it.

The steel roof trusses came in two parts, each about seventeen feet long. Two men carried one-half of a truss by setting an end on a large ball of banana leaves on their shoulders. The day before our departure we still needed four truss sections to form two complete trusses. The pastor told us that eight men from the church would leave at five in the morning to make their way down the mountain and return with what we needed to finish the job. Right on schedule, at five o'clock the next day, we awoke to the sound of conversation as the men assembled outside of the house in which we slept. The pastor's wife, a feisty woman in her sixties, questioned the wisdom of sending one of the men down the mountain. "You are sending a boy to do a man's job," she said. As I lay in my sleeping bag and continued listening to the conversation, I heard her begin to pray. "Oh, God, you know how I would have loved to have been born a man, but here I am, an old woman. I can't do much. But I call on you, Heavenly Father, to give these men strength, strength to build your church. Give them safety on the road. I pray in your name. Amen."

In mid-afternoon we still needed one-half of a roof truss. Evidently, two of the men struggled to get back up the mountain. The pastor's wife quickly pointed out that one of the men was only a boy.

People kept watching for the men, hoping we could finish the job. A cheer went up when the forty people at the church that day saw them come over a hill. When the two men heard the encouragement of their friends, they began to run. They kept running up the last hill, about seventy-five yards, before they collapsed at the top.

No runner has ever received a more enthusiastic greeting at the end of a marathon. I joined the laughter and clapping and cheering. These two men came in last place, but they finished the race . . . just in time. I rejoiced when I saw that the pastor's wife joined the celebration too.

Chapter 8

Baby Blue

A single finger cannot catch a flea.

~ Haitian Proverb

Preparation for market day in Dessalines, Haiti, started before sunrise. Early on Wednesdays and Saturdays, the "killing house" next to the orphanage started the messy work of preparing meat for the market. Our guests often wanted to watch the Haitian way to slaughter an animal.

The meat cutters tied the head of a goat to a tree. When they slit the throat, they caught the blood to drink later. A poor woman who lived nearby often stopped by in hopes of getting a little nourishment.

When the goat was sufficiently bled, they tied a small rope around the neck like a tourniquet. Then they made a small incision on the skin at the lower part of the shank of a back leg. One person blew through the slit in the skin like inflating a balloon. With a piece of rebar, they beat the skin like a drum until the skin fully separated from the body. Thump. Thump. In about four minutes the goat looked ready for the Thanksgiving Day parade in New York City. The loosened skin easily came off of the goat.

When the goat had been gutted, one person took the intestines to the spring about two hundred yards away for cleaning while another used a tree trunk as a chopping block. A machete reduced the carcass to small pieces about the size of a man's thumb, meat and bones together. These small pieces were stuffed into the cleaned intestines like ground pork and spices fill casing to make Italian sausage. The butchers could fit a whole goat into the intestines. They coiled the stuffed, bulging intestines in a large wash pan to carry to market.

As the butchers finished preparing for the market, up to two hundred other vendors flooded the streets. Since other villages held market day on Tuesdays and Fridays, one vendor could work four days a week by going to different towns. When the trucks carrying the vendors and merchandise rumbled into Dessalines, a cloud of dust settled over the town. A vendor would spread a twelve-foot square, plastic tarp on the ground to display the wares for sale.

Market days were always chaotic. Truck horns, babies crying, and vendors shouting at would-be customers created a surge of sound. Sometimes we heard a thud followed by a dog yipping; the dog snuck up behind a vendor looking for food only to be sent scampering away with a swat.

One crazy woman added to the frenzied life at the market. She might have been fifty years old and weighed less than one hundred pounds. Once she spotted her prey, she would sneak up behind them, jump on their back, and smother them with a bear hug. Then she cackled like a deranged old woman from a fairy tale. She was strong; people had difficulty getting loose from her stranglehold. Every ten minutes or so, you would hear yelling and laughter that indicated she caught a new victim.

Vendors bartered with every potential customer. No one had fixed prices. Sometimes the process went on and on. For example, when someone asked about buying some meat, the seller would draw several inches of the meat-stuffed intestine over the edge of the wash pan. The woman would move the knife along the intestine until she knew how much meat the person wanted to buy. Once they agreed on a price, the woman cut the portion and let it fall on a banana leaf or newspaper. The buyer would not know exactly what was purchased until the buyer squeezed the meat out of the intestine into a cooking pot. Most people purchased meat and bone about the size of a chicken egg to be used mostly for flavoring.

Shela and Sher'ri developed the ability to barter effectively. Once when the girls were helping a work team do some shopping, they overheard a vendor say, "Be careful with that white girl. She speaks Creole and she is tough like a coconut in getting the best price." I like that—tough like a coconut. I still laugh at that memory.

In the spring of 1984, our family faced a decision about what to do next. We had lived in Haiti for five years. Shela was about to graduate from high school, so this seemed like a good time to return to the United States where we could help her get started in college. That would allow Sher'ri to finish high school in Oregon. Karen and I could be closer to our extended families and friends.

But something festered in me that formed the primary reason for my consideration of returning to the United States. We could tell our friends that it was because of the girls, an acceptable excuse, when in reality I faced a personal crisis. I felt an intense anger toward God for all of the suffering I witnessed. The political climate in Haiti at the time seemed to increase the misery. In spite of all my effort, even though I worked long days and fell into bed bone tired every night, I could not see that we made any progress. God had gone AWOL. If only God would step in and do something! As hard as I tried, I failed to accomplish much that seemed to slow the downhill slide. I did not like the feeling of failure; I would just go home.

So when a doctor and a donor asked to meet me about building a hospital in a rural part of Haiti, I leaned toward saying no. I was not inclined to take on a new project at that time. The polite response to the invitation was to meet these two men for lunch, so I agreed to join them at a hotel in Port-au-Prince. I went to lunch with a bit of sadness knowing that I would likely tell them of our plan to return to the United States.

The hotel sat on the mountainside overlooking the city. You could see the airport and the ocean from our table outside near the pool. The servers in white jackets brought us soft drinks served over ice, not the typical way of doing things in many of the places I had visited in Haiti.

The two men quickly filled me in on the details. The donor was ready to pay for the construction of a hospital that the doctor would operate. They had asked three people who they should get to lead the construction and all three mentioned me.

When they said that the hospital would be constructed in Dessalines, my mind immediately went into overdrive. I knew Dessalines, having lived there for five weeks with the Teen Mission team in 1978 and then six months in 1979 when we ran the orphanage.

As we talked, I visualized the pigs and goats roaming freely, eating from the piles of garbage along the streets. They only had two places to get water, one the open spring near the orphanage and the other a half-inch water pipe near the market. I had watched as families sent kids with one-gallon jugs to get water, often pushing and shoving to get a turn to put the jug under the spigot. The meek may inherit the earth, but they go home with no water.

I also knew about the great need for health care in Dessalines. During our six-month stay at the orphanage in 1979, one day at lunch I said that what the people of Dessalines really needed was a hospital. A hospital would reduce the need for the orphanage. We were doing the right thing in caring for these children, I said, but the real need was to do something about parents who died because of a lack of medical care.

On market day in Dessalines, vendors show up to help sick people, carrying a suitcase filled with medicine and syringes. I have watched a vendor swirl the needle in a glass of water, pull the plunger up and down several times to rinse out the barrel, and shake the rinsed syringe in the air to dry it so they would be ready for the next person who needed an injection. I once asked a medicine vendor where he got his pills. He told me that his brother in Port-au-Prince supplied the medicine. "If it burns when you go peepee," he said, "you take this green one. If you have the 'grip' (flu-like symptoms), you take these yellow ones. And if you are very ill, I give you a 'pickie' (an injection of a milky colored liquid)." What a deal, a person could come to market with a fever and go home with HIV.

Almost daily when we lived in Dessalines, people asked us for medical assistance. I once tried to help a man with a serious cut on his foot. Without a painkiller, I closed the wound with five ugly stitches. Another time a man complained of a tooth-ache. His breath smelled awful and I could clearly see two abscessed teeth. So I gave the man some money, wrote a note in which I promised to pay the balance, and sent the man to a dentist twenty-five miles away. Later that afternoon the man returned, spitting blood between each sentence. The dentist had removed seven teeth. The next morning he complained about not sleeping well and having a headache. His face was so swollen his eyes were almost shut.

The two men who invited me to lunch had a great dream. I knew my friends in Dessalines desperately needed the kind of care they could provide. But I also knew the challenges of building in a place like that. Few skilled workers lived in the area. Most of the people in Dessalines lived in mud huts, not concrete-block houses. Building supplies would have to be trucked to the town over rough roads. This would not be easy.

I left the lunch meeting with my mind spinning. They needed a hospital, dental office, pharmacy, storage, five apartments for healthcare workers, a water system, and sewage treatment. Not convinced that I should be involved, I still agreed to go to Dessalines to check out the situation. I could not openly discuss the idea with anyone—political leaders expected to make a major announcement like this whether they had anything to do with the development or not.

I wanted my family to join me on this trip. It might be the last time we could visit the orphans and orphanage workers in Dessalines. I proposed that we leave early on a Saturday morning. It took us four hours; the last hour involved traveling only ten miles. It was hot and we had no air conditioning in the car. Dust drifted through the open windows as we moved down the bumpy road. The payoff would come partway home when we stopped at a resort for a swim in the ocean and a meal.

We had reached the end of our exploratory trip to Dessalines. We finished our visit with friends at the orphanage and returned to our car. What we saw next started a chain of experiences that made the future clearly visible.

A carpenter shop sits next to the "killing house." About ten feet square, the carpenter used the shed to store lumber and hand tools. He worked in front of the shed, under a low flat roof to shield him from the sun, on a workbench about the size of a ping-pong table. Lumber would be ripped and planed by hand. The carpenter made mostly tables, chairs, and caskets.

As we climbed into our car, we watched a young man leaving the carpenter shop, carrying a small casket, something for a child of three years or younger. The carpenter painted the casket baby blue with purple trim. After living outside of the United States for twenty years, I do not recall ever seeing a child's casket, certainly not in a rural area like Dessalines. In Haiti, most families wrap the child's body in a beach towel or white cotton sheet. But this father likely paid two weeks' wages for a casket for his child.

The man carried the casket like someone carrying a sheet cake into a wedding reception hall, not like a sack of flour on a hip or shoulder. The paint may have still been wet. He walked slowly with his eyes focused straight ahead. Occasionally he looked down at the casket, but his eyes never shifted to those of us who watched. He seemed to walk in a dome of silence that settled over him to shut out market day noise. No one greeted him. He took step after step on his lonely journey.

I have known other Haitians who buried a child. As they dug the grave, they worked quietly with no expression of outward emotion. No jokes. No talking. No sobbing. Sometimes a parent might be subdued for weeks following the death of a child.

This man came to Dessalines on market day for a quiet, solemn transaction instead of noisy bartering punctuated with laughter. The transaction took place in a small carpenter shop instead of the public marketplace.

Before we headed for the resort, we stopped to visit with Snowball, a very old man who had become our friend. We helped him rid his house of bedbugs and lice. Sometimes we shared food with him. He had lived in Dallas, Texas, for a while, and was one of only a few people in Dessalines who spoke English. While in Texas, he constantly complained about the cold weather, so his friends started calling him Snowball.

One day Snowball gave me some advice. "If you want to be old like me with white hair," he said, "when people ask you about government issues, you tell them, 'Some people say this, some say that, but for me, I don't know who to believe.'" Snowball learned how to survive in the politically charged atmosphere of Haiti in the 1980s.

While we talked with Snowball, we heard the crunch of gravel as someone walked nearby. Snowball paid no attention to the stranger in town, but we saw that it was the young father carrying the baby blue casket.

We made one last stop before heading out of town, the hillside where apartments would be built. From our vantage point we could see rice fields in the valley, palm trees, and the foothills leading to the mountains that rose a few thousand feet over Dessalines.

That is when we saw the man for the third time. By now he was high in the foothills, about a half-mile away. No trees blocked our view. We watched in silence as he trudged up a thirty-degree incline. At this point we saw just a speck of blue, but we knew the man carried a casket. We knew a young child had died.

None of us said a word as we watched the man climb higher. Only poor folks lived in the mountains away from the main source of water. Was this man making a personal statement about the worth of a child?

I stood quietly as the young father carried the casket so tenderly up the hillside.

"Dad"—Shela spoke first—"if you built a hospital here, maybe he would never again have to bury his child."

Tears of grief took the young father out of view. We turned to each other. Arms and tears mixed together in a family hug.

I do not recall looking back up the mountain. I suppose the man continued the slow march to his house, placed his child's body in the casket, lowered the casket into the ground, covered the casket with dirt, and comforted the child's mother.

We did not look back because we had already turned toward a new day. For the next two years we worked with the unwavering conviction that we could actually do something about the suffering experienced by people in and around that rural Haitian town.

We went to Dessalines on market day looking for confirmation about our intention to leave Haiti. Instead, we returned to Port-au-Prince with a mission.

Chapter 9

Joy Required

Roaches are never right when facing chickens.
~ Haitian Proverb

O nce permission had been granted for the construction of the Claire Heureuse Hospital in Dessalines,
I purchased a yellow dump truck and a sixteen-foot,
tandem-axle trailer and began moving building materials. I
could not talk about the project with anyone since the official
announcement had yet to be made, but I went to work anyway. An old man watched me as I unloaded my trailer one day.
"Does Dessalines have a hospital?" I asked the man.

"No," he quickly replied.

"Maybe the government in Port-au-Prince will come soon
to build a hospital."

The man laughed, clearly hearing my words with a degree
of cynicism. "The people in Port-au-Prince do not even know
we exist," he said. "We will never have a hospital here until the
evangelicals come."

"I'm an evangelical," I told the man. I wanted so much to
add that the evangelicals would soon build a hospital on this
very site. I never saw the old man again. I looked for him. I

wanted to remind him about what he told me and confirm that he had accurately described the care provided by evangelical Christians.

Once we started construction, each week I employed twenty-five men. Eight workers had experience and skills, so they worked every week. I used these men to run the concrete mixer, weld, and lay blocks. The other seventeen workers functioned as laborers, pushing wheelbarrows, digging ditches, and shoveling sand and gravel into the concrete mixer. Every Monday, I hired a different group of laborers to work for the week. This allowed many families in Dessalines to benefit from the construction project. I paid the workers $2.00 per day when the going rate at the time was $1.70 per day. We worked from eight in the morning to five in the afternoon. This allowed the workers time to tend to their gardens before sunset.

I had worked with Francine before, so he became a key assistant with the hospital construction. One day Francine brought Little John with him to the work site. The ten-year-old's father had died and his mother had mental issues. Little John and his mother relied totally on neighbors to care for them. Francine told me that it would be better to have Little John at the work site where Francine could watch him rather than just allow him to run the streets.

I soon discovered that Little John anticipated what someone needed to keep working. If Little John heard a dump truck coming with a load of sand, he went to the storeroom to get the shovels. If he saw a mason needed more mortar, without being told Little John got a bucket of mud and dumped it on the mason's board. I bought a small trowel so Little John could learn to lay concrete blocks.

I will never forget the day Little John counted the soda bottles and realized that there was one for him. That day he knew he belonged to the group. I began paying him half of what I paid the adult workers.

We ran into a problem when we dug the foundation for the five-unit apartment building that would be used by hospital personnel. We quickly discovered that very little soil covered boulders the size of a car. To get the foundation deep enough on the steep terrain, I wanted to dig down more than the rock allowed. One day I told the workers to expose the top of a boulder and to build a fire that we kept burning through the night. In the morning we dumped cold water on the hot rock. I was confident that the rock would break, but only a little bit sloughed off.

Another day I dusted off a rock about three feet across and saw a potential crack. I took the sixteen-pound sledgehammer that had a handle made of the rear axle from a truck. Four men watched as I hit the rock five or six times. When the rock began to split, I handed the sledgehammer to one man and said in Creole, "Do it like that."

The man replied, "I could be strong like you if I had food to eat."

I had nothing to say to the man at that moment. I provided employment in a town where jobs were hard to find. I did what I could, but the need exceeded what I could do. I grieved at my inadequacy to do everything that needed to be done.

Since we had trouble with the rocks where we wanted to build the apartments, we eventually changed our plans and incorporated the boulders into the foundation. Dégagé. Once we swept and rinsed the boulder so that all dirt had been removed, we spread mud on the big rock and started laying blocks. The front of that apartment building has a rock-solid foundation.

One evening after work, a regular worker came to my two-room house and told me his daughter had died. I had heard the news the previous week. I told him how sorry I was at his loss. He asked if he could borrow a shovel to dig the grave. This confused me since I knew his daughter's body had already been buried. He added that he could use a pick too since the ground was hard. I told him that I did not understand. Then he told me that a second daughter just died. I went to the storeroom to loan him the tools. He walked about twenty feet, tools in hand, then turned to ask if he could borrow money for a small place in the cemetery where he could bury his daughter. I gave him the money; it was not a loan.

I went into my house and sat on the edge of my cot. *How can a man bury two daughters within a week? What is his wife doing while he digs the grave, alone, as the dark of night approaches?* I thought of my own two daughters when they were eight and ten years old. As I sat surrounded by extremely poor people who faced difficulty and death day after day, I had more questions than answers.

Four nights a week for two years I had restless sleep. In the summer months I felt the sweat tickle my skin as it ran onto my mattress. I usually went to bed by nine thirty. About midnight I moved my head to the other end of the bed so my upper body would have a dry sheet. That cooled me down a bit. At least once in the night I would get up, open the door, and step into the night air to cool off. Of course I closed the door behind me. I did not want mosquitoes on the inside of my house, irritating me with the constant buzz. When one snuck in, I laid in bed and slapped at the nuisance. Do you know how hard it is to hit a mosquito in the dark? Even a flashlight provided little aid in tracking down the little dive bombers when they got inside the house.

About every ten days the Vodou (Voodoo) priest who lived across from my house held a service in which the participants invited the spirits to take possession of them. Sometimes the ceremony lasted six hours, continuing until four in the morning. On nights when I could not sleep, I often stood behind a fence, undetected, about twenty feet from where they beat the drum. I stared at the priest as he dropped bones on the ground, and then made predictions for the future based on how the bones landed. I watched the alcohol-fueled frenzy as some of the men who worked on the hospital danced to the drumbeat. I heard women shriek in a high pitch as the evil spirits came on them.

In the cool night air, as I stood alone in the darkness, I wept for my friends. I prayed that the Light would come. I have seen the power of evil. But I have also seen the liberation that comes to those who believe in Jesus as their Savior, to those filled with the Holy Spirit. When the drum beating and dancing stopped, I would go back to my house to try to rest a bit more before sunrise.

One day the chief of police came to visit me. He had heard about me and wanted to meet me. "I didn't realize you were so short," he said after introducing himself.

I took the tape measure from my belt and put it around the police officer's waist. "I didn't know you were so fat," I replied. He laughed.

The police chief liked me. My good relationship with this guy surprised Snowball who called the chief the meanest man in Haiti. I stopped by the police station one day, and since I did not see anyone in the front of the station, I walked into the part of the building where they had the jail cells. When the chief found me wandering through the building, he quickly escorted me out. He said, "It is not good for you to see the jail. Too much blood." I knew of persons who died in police custody in those days, so I understood the full extent of the police chief's statement.

We did not have any problem with theft from the hospital construction site. Even when the shipping container arrived with medical equipment and supplies valued at two hundred thousand dollars, no one took a thing. I wonder if people knew that the police chief considered me his friend and if that was enough of a deterrent to prevent people from even thinking about stealing from the hospital.

The Free Methodist pastor came to me one day to talk about construction process. "May I have per-mission to give you counsel?" he asked.

"Of course," I replied. I had the highest regard for this man.

"I have been watching. Everyone is happy with the hospital but you." He paused a moment, then continued. "You are in a hurry. You chastise the workers because you feel like they are deliberately dragging their feet so the employment lasts longer."

"But people are dying," I said. "We need to finish building the hospital as soon as we can."

"Yes," the pastor replied, "people are dying. And they will die after this hospital is in operation." Then he said, "Swanee, you must understand that the people of Dessalines are happy to have this hospital. They are happy to see the progress, to see it happening. *When* it gets done is only important to you. Right now, everyone is happy except Swanee."

Those were hard words for me to hear, but I received them with the same grace by which they were spoken. I knew I needed to change. I needed to think differently. I needed to modify what I said and how I structured the workday.

Years later, in Kericho, Kenya, I had a videotape of Mother Teresa where she said that joy is required when serving the poor. I watched that tape a dozen times, often with Bible college students. I believe Mother Teresa spoke the truth. I began to learn that lesson after the pastor talked with me in Dessalines.

About that time I stopped taking photographs of the building projects. I had a nice camera with several specialty lenses. I had taken a photography course at the community college in Oregon, so I could make well-composed photos. I knew how to position myself so you could see the straight walls. I used lenses to make the building seem larger and more striking. In the early years I had good photos with which to impress the people in the United States about the excellent work I did in less than ideal circumstances. But something changed within me. Buildings did not seem to be as important to me as they had been, so I stopped taking photos.

If we had a full day of work at the hospital, like a large concrete pour, I ordered food for everyone. A woman prepared a large kettle of rice and beans. She pulled apart the layers of paper in a cement sack and used a clean piece of paper as a plate. Mostly for show and maybe a little bit of flavor, the cook dropped small cubes of pork on top of the food in the kettle.

When we stopped to eat, everyone expected the cook to serve me first. She always made sure I got a piece of pork. One time the meat on my paper included part of the skin with hair sticking out at least an inch. Lots of hair. So I picked up the pork by the hair and dropped it on the paper held by the worker next to me. The workers saw what had happened, and knew I would always be served a piece of pork, so they started trying to sit beside me at mealtime. I caught on to what they were doing. So after everyone was settled to eat, I started getting up and walking across the circle to give the meat to another worker. Everyone laughed at the game.

A couple of days a week I ordered a cornmeal pudding cake. The cook used bananas to flavor the cornmeal cake cooked in a flat pan. She cut the cake into two-inch pieces and served it on six-inch squares of cement bag paper. The sweet, gooey cake, usually still warm, provided a treat for the workers.

In those days I learned to value process, of traveling together. My tendency to look primarily at the project and not the people needed to change. I began to believe that my workers needed me as a friend and companion as much as they needed the job I provided.

Chapter 10

Bless Me!

Words have wings.

~ Haitian Proverb

On one of my many trips moving building materials from Port-au-Prince to Dessalines, a group of boys gathered to watch me unload concrete blocks. These boys lived in houses nearby, temporary structures on land that I suspect belonged to someone other than the occupants. These families were squatters.

As I unloaded the blocks from the trailer, I asked the boys to help me. Each concrete block weighed about thirty pounds, but these boys had enough strength to carry a block of that size. I handed them the blocks and they carried the blocks to where I had started a stack.

As we neared the end of the load, I slid the blocks to the back of the flatbed trailer where the boys grabbed them. A boy of eight or nine years reached to pick up a block at the same moment that I slid another down the trailer. The middle finger on his right hand lay over the top of the block when the second block slid into it and smashed the end of his finger. He cried out in pain, but never shed a tear. I quickly went back to look at his finger. He was really hurt; the end of his finger above the fingernail was smashed, the skin torn and twisted. It began to bleed.

During those years in Haiti I always carried a well-stocked first-aid kit in my truck. I hurried to get the kit and began to work on his finger. I poured drinking water slowly over his hand while he cleaned the wound with his other hand. (I always had the other person do this so I would not have contact with the blood.) When it was clean, we washed it again with antibiotic soap. The finger continued to bleed so we just let the blood drop on the ground. Then I wrapped the finger in clean gauze and he held it tightly to stop the bleeding. All the time we worked on his finger, I assured him how sorry I was that he hurt his finger. After the initial cry, this little boy never made another sound. With his finger wrapped in a clean, white bandage, we began to talk.

My little friend got right to the point. "You hurt me," he said, "and now you have to pay." Just think, he made this announcement without talking to his attorney. By this time about fifteen people gathered around us.

As I wrapped his finger, I had been thinking that he smashed his finger while working on his own hospital. So I told him my thoughts.

"No," he said to me, "this is your hospital. You're the one building it."

"I'm building this hospital for *you*," I said, "and everyone else in Dessalines." My statement did not satisfy the boy, so I switched my approach. "If I get hurt," I said, "really hurt, where will I go to the hospital?"

"Port-au-Prince," he said without hesitation.

"You are correct," I said. "Now if I am very sick, so sick I might die, where will I go to the hospital?"

"United States," he said.

"Which hospital will you go to?"

The look on his face told me he understood my point. "Here," he said softly. "I live here."

I told my little friend that he injured his hand working on his own hospital. The crowd listened intently to our conversation.

"Who is going to pay me for building your hospital?" I demanded. When no one responded, I asked the question again. "Who is going to pay me? Look, I've been working hard on *your* hospital and I'm thirsty. No one has given me water to drink." I showed them my dirty hands. "No one has even given me water to wash my hands. Who is going to pay me? I'm building this hospital for you and you and you." I pointed to various people as I said that phrase.

"I have nothing," the boy said.

"But you have to pay me," I demanded. "I'm building this hospital *for you*."

I hardly finished saying this when the boy dived forward and grabbed me in a big bear hug around my waist. As he clung tightly to me, I put my arms around his head. I held his wiry hair close to my chest. He seemed as comfortable hugging me as I was being hugged. When we finally broke the embrace, I had tears on my cheeks. I told him again in front of the whole group how sorry I was that he got hurt. I was truly sorry.

In the next two years, this boy and I hugged each other many times. I learned to love these little ragtag boys who lived next door to me. I gently touched all of them if they were close enough for me to reach.

As the local first-aid man, on some days I went to my first-aid kit often to assist someone. One day I watched a young boy messing with the shinbone on one of his legs. At first I could not make sense out of what I saw. After asking several questions, I discovered that the boy had filled a deep wound with dry cement. Over time the wound healed with the ball of hard cement deep in his flesh. I put ointment where the wound had been and wrapped it in gauze. I told the boy to come see me the next day. Over several days I was able to soften the tissue enough to pick out the cement plug.

I began hiring these boys to help me prepare for the next day's work. After my workers left in the late afternoon, I negotiated with the boys for that evening's jobs. For example, I paid them to move sand from where the truck dumped it to where the workers would use it to mix concrete or mortar. They carried concrete blocks when a new delivery arrived. I always had them straighten up the job site: stack wood scraps, gather broken blocks into one pile, rake sand into mounds. The boys working in the evening made it possible for my workers to immediately begin their jobs the next morning.

After I got the boys working, I put on my swimsuit and headed for the spring. In one pocket I carried a small bottle of shampoo; in the other a bar of soap. I dropped my towel at the edge of the spring and, still wearing my tennis shoes and swimsuit, walked into the spring up to my chest to bathe. When I returned to my house, I changed into short pants to go inspect the work of the boys. I paid them daily.

During the time I worked on the hospital in Dessalines, I often suffered with "Haitian happiness," also known as Montezuma's revenge, the trots, and diarrhea. In one five-week stretch I lost twenty-two pounds. On one morning I hurried to the pit latrine two hundred yards from the work site for the third time, and we were only halfway to lunch. The hot Caribbean sun turned the outhouse with a tin roof into a one-man oven. I groaned with my arms folded over my tummy.

Just about five feet from where I sat, several young boys played a game similar to jacks. They tossed a stone and attempted to scoop up one smaller stone while the tossed stone was still in the air. If they succeeded, they tossed the stone again and tried to snatch two smaller stones, and so on. While they played their game, I heard one boy say, "You know, white people make a lot of poop."

They had my attention.

"Yea, I know," his buddy replied. "They eat too much."

I walked to the latrine in a hurry with a grimace on my face, but returned to work with a smile.

These boys did not attend school. A few years before, I sat in a pickup truck in Dumay, Haiti, after the dedication of a new school building. I wept as I sat alone. I knew that only a small percentage of the children in the valley of sugar cane fields would get to attend this school. Memories of my own elementary school experiences came to mind. Since I could not read until I was ten years old, teachers accused me of being lazy and daydreaming in class. I loathed staying inside while my friends played outside during recess. I wanted to run, but I had to sit at my desk. I did not even know the word dyslexia until I attended college, and only then began to understand the source my frustrations in grade school. Clearly, I never would have been in school if I had been raised in Haiti. Perhaps my love for the boys in Dessalines, boys who likely never would know the joy of reading or have the ability to do math, maybe they reminded me of myself as a boy.

In those two years in Dessalines, I rented a two-room house for three hundred dollars a year. I had two chairs and one small table, an army cot with a night-stand beside it. My only luxury was a six-inch electric fan that I powered with an electric cord strung through the window and into the dump truck. I only used the fan to get cool enough to go to sleep. Sometime in the night I unplugged it so as not to run down the truck battery.

One evening when I parked the dump truck on the side of the house, I noticed several empty cement sacks in the back of the truck. I usually gave the sacks to women in town who took them apart to reuse the paper. On this evening, since the boys were nearby, I asked if they wanted the cement sacks. A fight broke out as the boys grabbed for the sacks. They swung elbows and threw punches. I grabbed the boy closest to me. "What's going on?" I hollered.

"I want these," the boy replied.

"I see that. Why fight over cement sacks?"

"I want this paper to sleep on tonight. The ground is cold."

I did not know the boys slept on the dirt. I asked my workers the next day how many had a mattress to sleep on. Only two men of the twenty-five raised their hands. Most slept on grass mats.

One evening when I returned to my house, I watched a young child use a stick to dig burnt cornmeal from the bottom of a cooking pot that had sat over an open flame. This child, about five years old, worked diligently for dry, black crumbs.

I went into my house, shut the door, and locked it. I opened my ice chest to get dinner. I ate alone.

"Rescue those who are unjustly sentenced to death; don't stand back and let them die. Don't try to disclaim responsibility by saying you didn't know about it. For God, who knows all hearts, knows yours, and he knows you knew!" (Prov. 24:11–12 TLB).

When I read those words in Seattle years before, I knew considerably less about those unjustly sentenced to death than I did as I sat locked in my house in Dessalines. I knew what happened right outside my door. I knew about the hunger. I knew about the suffering. I knew about fathers who buried children. And I knew that God knew that I knew.

The weight of responsibility weighed heavy on me. I sometimes look back on those days and regret that I did not fill my house with the children instead of shutting them out. I regret that I did not feed them, even if it consisted only of white bread and warm soda.

But then I remember how very tired I felt on many of those evenings. I knew the injustice, and I gladly accepted my responsibility, but I did not have the strength to do more. None. I sat on my bed and told God of my frustrations, my awareness of the great need, my anguish that I could not do more to change the circumstances in which these boys, my friends, lived. I wept with the pain of seeing such pervasive suffering but feeling helpless to do much about it.

I felt lonely, too. I wanted to be with Karen and Sher'ri. I looked forward to the weekends when I went to Port-au-Prince. I loved doing things with my friends. On Monday mornings, when I climbed into the yellow dump truck for the four-hour trip to Dessalines, I became aware of just how deeply the fatigue penetrated my body. I drove toward another week of strenuous days, of evenings alone, of sitting in my small house and feeling overwhelmed by the needs all around me.

I lived simply. But just a few feet away my young friends slept on cement sacks. They scavenged for food. I saw so many people who were sick and dying that I knew I had to muster the strength somehow to work another day. Then another. From somewhere deep within, I needed to arouse enough energy to do what I could, even if I became totally spent in the process. I failed in my attempt to change Haiti, but ultimately understood that God did not call me to be successful in that effort. God called me to be a man of compassion, to suffer with those who suffer.

Karen and I returned to Dessalines for a visit about fifteen years after we left Haiti. We rented a car in Port-au-Prince and drove to Dessalines. When we came into town, people recognized me. They ran alongside of the car chanting "Swanee, Swanee, Swanee." When we stopped at the hospital, people gathered around wanting to shake my hand. We were so glad to see our friends again. We saw the hospital running at full capacity. We met people who would have died if it had not been for the Claire Heureuse Hospital.

We rejoiced that we played a part in bringing healthcare to Dessalines.

When we left the hospital, I drove to the hillside where we constructed the five-unit apartment building. I honked the car horn at the steel gate and the watchman came out to see what I wanted. I recognized the man even though I had not seen him in years. This man had been one of the little boys I hired to help in the evenings. We were far enough away from the hospital that the watchman did not see the commotion when we drove into town earlier that day.

"Do you know who I am?" I asked.

"No," he replied.

I let him look at me a moment, then I said, "I'm Swanee."

This man began to jump and yell like he did when he was a little boy. Quick as a cat, he grabbed both of my wrists, lifted my hands to the top of his head, and rubbed my hands in his curly hair. As he did this, he called out, "Bless me! Bless me! Bless me!"

What a moment of joy! Karen and the two friends who traveled with us joined me in laughing with pure delight. Some might have looked on that scene and ridiculed the child-like behavior. I felt affirmed in that moment.

As we continued the conversation, this man thanked me for giving him small jobs when he was a boy. He said that the only money he had as a child came from what I paid him to carry a few concrete blocks or rake sand into a pile. He said that the money he brought home helped feed his family.

I had given the boys what most Americans would consider pocket change. I did not know that the little bit I did was all the income some families had. As I listened to my young friend, I realized that what seemed so small to me at the time made a difference for a few families. I may not have saved the world, or even the whole town of Dessalines, but I helped a few boys. Maybe that was enough.

Chapter 11

Roadblock

A silk dress does not mean the
underwear is clean.
~ Haitian Proverb

A fter I began building the Claire Heureuse Hospital in Dessalines, Karen had plenty of time on her hands, so she started a women's Bible study. When Karen invited the mother of a classmate of Sher'ri's to attend the Bible study, she said yes. Karen's friend even suggested that the group meet in her home. The friendship between Karen and her friend continued until eventually we spent many weekends sharing a meal with Karen's friend and her family.

One weekend, the friend's husband called to ask Karen and me to join him for dinner with one of his best customers at the manufacturing plant he owned. His wife was out of the country and he wanted company for this business dinner. He told us to meet him at the most expensive restaurant in Haiti. Since our car sat in the repair shop, the only transportation we had was the yellow dump truck. So Karen and I got all dressed up in our fanciest clothes, climbed into the cab of the dump truck, and drove to the swanky restaurant.

Just about the time we ordered our meal, the president of Haiti and his wife walked in. This was a time of great political unrest, so with the president came bodyguards carrying automatic weapons. As we ate our dinner, I looked straight ahead at the table where the president sat no more than twelve feet away. A third person sat at the table, a man who looked exactly like the president. I could identify the real president from the body double by the way he interacted with his wife. Karen and I enjoyed the meal, but the atmosphere was unnerving.

As we said goodbye to our friend, he asked where we had parked. "Around the corner," I told him. Karen and I walked down the street and climbed into the dump truck for the ride to our house.

Part of the reason for the political unrest in those days involved Haitian leaders who used their power for personal benefit. One day, as I worked on the second floor of the apartments in Dessalines, a big, black SUV stopped in the roadway in front of the building. Four well-dressed men got out and called out a greeting. I really did not want to go down to talk with these men, but I did. I asked Francine to go with me. One of the men identified himself as a deputy (similar to a United States senator) serving the Dessalines region. He offered greetings from the Haitian president and thanked me for all I had done to help the Haitian people. Then he began to speak about a road project between Dessalines and another village in the mountains.

I began to be suspicious of what he told me.

The man pulled out a paper with a list of materials they needed: four hundred gallons of diesel oil, cement, plywood, lumber, ceiling board.

The last item made me think that these materials would be used to build a house, not a road. I told the deputy that the hospital would not participate in the project.

The man's expression seemed like I had just tossed ice water in his face. The deputy took a step toward me and with exaggerated articulation said, "I don't think I am hearing you!"

Oh, my. I had gone too far to back up. I told the deputy and his friends that I only served as the building supervisor and that I did not sit on the board of directors for the hospital. Therefore, I pointed out, I did not have authority to give away what belonged to hospital.

"You see," the deputy attempted to reason with me, "your development work and our development work are all for the same purpose."

"I will present your request to the board of directors," I said. "When we finish with the construction of the hospital, if we have remaining building materials perhaps the board of directors will approve your request."

"You have keys to everything," the deputy said. "You could give me whatever you wanted to from the storeroom."

When I refused to budge, the deputy told us that they would return. They walked to the SUV in a huff, slammed the doors, and took off with the spinning wheels tossing loose gravel like machine gun fire.

I knew how the system worked. I once had a man get very angry with me when I refused his help. He told me to give him a list of building materials and in a few days he would make the delivery. When I tried to politely change the subject, he pushed harder. He wanted to help me, he insisted, but I knew his methods. "It's just not right to build churches with stolen materials," I told him. The Haitians who overheard the conversation laughed when I said that.

We watched as the deputy and his henchmen created a trail of dust. Francine spoke for the first time and said that the deputy was a "big man" in the government. He told me that this man had a brother with a gun. Once before when a Catholic priest refused a similar shakedown, Francine said, the brother fired the gun into the ground right behind the priest as he walked away.

I was scared. I went back to the job site and called the twenty-five men to gather around me. I explained again that we were constructing *their* hospital and I did not want the government to interfere. This "big man" wanted to take from the poor for his own enrichment. I told the workers to talk with their friends about what they witnessed. I figured that the more people who knew about the confrontation, the better for me. Then I asked them to protect me.

At this point, I had lived among the people of Dessalines for many months. I provided employment for scores of men and built goodwill among the people in multiple ways. The police chief was my friend. Even with all of these good relationships, I still felt afraid as I slept alone in my small house on dark nights.

I never saw the deputy again.

As was my habit for two years, I left Dessalines for Port-au-Prince on a Friday afternoon. Political tension had been building for a long time, but during the preceding week we heard reports in Dessalines of the chaos in Port-au-Prince. As I drove the dump truck away from Dessalines, I remembered a conversation I had the previous weekend with Elsie, the woman who worked in our house and stayed with Sher'ri when Karen and I hosted a work team. She told me that in previous times, the president of Haiti tossed money out of a moving car. People scrambled to grab what they could. Sometimes cars in the president's entourage ran over children trying to pick up some money. The previous day, Elsie said, a caravan of cars drove by, including the president's vehicle, tossing bread in plastic wrappers to the people. To my surprise, Elsie said that people left the bread where it landed. Hungry people walked on, leaving the bread in the street for cars to smash flat. "We're not dogs that he can feed by throwing food at us," Elsie reported the people had said. I recognized that the president had lost all support of the people.

About two hours into my trip to Port-au-Prince on that Friday afternoon, I came to a roadblock made of rocks, tires, and a telephone pole resting on two fifty-five gallon barrels. This barricade blocked the main highway to Port-au-Prince. About fifty men stood around the roadblock. I did not see any guns, although there may have been weapons nearby. I saw no car or motorcycle. I knew if I could get past the roadblock I could outrun these guys. If something went wrong, well, I could not predict what would happen.

I put the nose of the truck right up to the pole. Fifteen or twenty men came to my window and began to talk. I could tell they had been drinking. They told me that after they painted "kill Duvalier!" on the side of my truck in blue paint, I would be allowed to drive on to Port-au-Prince.

I immediately realized the danger I faced with their plan, so I began to negotiate with the men. "This truck belongs to the hospital in Dessalines," I said. "This truck is used to help poor people just like you. Please let me turn around and go back to the hospital." After several minutes of conversation, they agreed to remove the pole and let me turn around.

I had hoped for this moment. When the men lifted the pole off of the barrels, I sped away like a crazy man. I kept looking in my mirrors to see if anyone followed me. I wondered if someone had jumped in the back of the dump truck. I could not see in there as I drove.

I knew exactly where to hide. About ten minutes down the highway, I took a quick right and drove the dump truck down a one-lane, dirt road between fields of banana trees. I was familiar with the area because I helped build a small duplex on the ocean at the end of this road. Missionaries used this duplex as a rest house. I could find the key to let myself in. I always traveled with a small suitcase and ice chest, but I remembered that the owners had fully furnished the duplex and stocked the cabinets with food. The place had its own water supply. There were very few houses in this area and absolutely no road traffic. I was confident that the men at the roadblock would not find me. I could safely hide there.

I found a missionary couple already at the duplex. We did not have telephone connections with folks in Port-au-Prince, so I had no contact with Karen. If things were really bad, I knew friends would help Karen and Sher'ri in my absence. I desperately wanted to know what was happening in Port-au-Prince, but I did not know if I would encounter additional roadblocks, so I stayed put in hopes that things would settle down enough for me to make it home safely.

For three days I waited. I took naps; I did not realize how tired I had become. I read books and outdated magazines. I repaired a seawall that had started to crack. I began thinking that we needed to leave Haiti as soon as possible. We had completed the exterior of the hospital and just had a few things to do on the inside: a little bit of painting, installing light switch plates, other finish work. We had unloaded the container from Canada filled with supplies and medical equipment, so items already sat on the shelves ready for the hospital to open.

When I left Dessalines on that Friday afternoon, I expected to return on Monday. As I thought about leaving Haiti, I realized that if I had known this was my last trip, I would have returned to Port-au-Prince with my tools and the personal items from my house.

On the fourth morning in my hideout, about four o'clock in the morning, I started toward Port-au-Prince. As I eased the dump truck onto the highway, I wondered if I should have left earlier even though I crept from my hiding place in the dark. The sun rose as I approached Port-au-Prince. Normally, I encountered people everywhere in Haiti, even early in the morning. Usually while driving I had to be on the lookout for dogs and pedestrians. I found it spooky to be driving into Port-au-Prince with no one on the roads. I saw evidence of rioting: piles of burnt tires, debris.

When I arrived home, it seemed to me that Karen and Sher'ri lived with more stress and anxiety than I had in the preceding days. They could talk on the telephone and they knew details about the unrest. I discovered that Sher'ri's school had closed. Karen and Sher'ri could not leave the house since the streets were not safe.

I do not recall that we had much of a discussion about what we would do. We knew that we needed to leave Haiti as soon as possible. The good days of living in Haiti had passed. We spent exactly one week cleaning out our house. We packed a few items for shipping and sold or gave away the rest. I signed the title to our car and left it with a personal friend to sell for us when it was safe to do so.

We had no opportunity to say goodbye. I left Francine, the boys, and the construction workers in Dessalines fully expecting to see them again on Monday. When Sher'ri left school on her last day, she did not know it was her last day. She did not have the chance to say goodbye to teachers and friends. Karen's friends in the women's club, well, it was like we just evaporated.

Missionary Flights (MFI) usually flies DC-3s. Given the unusual circumstances, MFI had three open seats on a small plane that allowed us to carry only three small, light suitcases. A friend came to drive us to the airport. I wept as I watched Sher'ri and Elsie hug. Sher'ri delighted in making Elsie laugh. I loved watching Elsie settle down on the floor, her legs weak from laughing so hard. Sher'ri and Elsie mimicked commercials on Haitian television. Sher'ri and Elsie brought so much joy to our house. Now they held tightly to each other as they said goodbye.

Just seven minutes from the house, we remembered that we had intended to give Elsie an item, so we returned to the house. In the moments we had been gone, men had already climbed over the fence and looted the house. As we turned back toward the airport without retrieving the item, we realized the wisdom of our decision to leave Haiti. Just a couple of weeks prior, someone had poisoned Dudley, our Doberman watchdog. Someone had been watching our house. They likely knew my schedule—a yellow dump truck in a residential neighborhood is easy to track. We left at the right time.

When we arrived in Florida, Missionary Flights had made room reservations for us at a motel. We called Karen's uncle who lived three hundred fifty miles away and asked him to come get us. Then we fell into bed, exhausted, but glad to be in a safe place.

The next morning we turned on the television in our motel room and saw the news bulletin that the Haitian president and his wife boarded a private plane soon after we left Haiti. In the days that followed, I often told people that when the president heard that we had left Haiti, he said to his wife, "Let's get out of here. This place will totally fall apart without Swanee, Karen, and Sher'ri."

As we prepared to leave Haiti, we packed about twelve hundred pounds of personal items and paid a freight forwarder to ship the crates to Oregon. While we were still in Florida, a friend called us to say that he found our photos dumped on a downtown street in Port-au-Prince. He picked up a small sack of our personal items. He said that it looked like all of our things had been stolen, that thieves used part of a telephone pole as a battering ram to break through the concrete block wall of the warehouse. He was right; we lost everything in the warehouse. Fortunately, the woman who handled the freight had our small, hand-carved chest of drawers and a steel drum filled with personal items at her house. She held the items there until the rioting stopped about forty-five days later. We were back in Portland when we received her telephone call saying that our things were on the way.

When I went to the cargo terminal at the Portland airport, I had a happy heart as I started for home with the shipment in the back of my pickup truck. Karen and I eagerly opened the barrel to discover that someone at the Port-au-Prince airport had removed all of the screws I used to secure the lid, taken our personal items, filled the barrel with old magazines, broken glass, airline shipping documents, pieces of cardboard, and dirt swept off of the floor at the Port-au-Prince airport, and meticulously replaced all of the screws.

I set the lid back on top of the barrel and walked away. I did not touch it for days; it just sat on our carport.

All we have left from the years we lived in Haiti is a hand-carved chest of drawers . . . and thousands of stories.

Chapter 12

Partners

They tried to bury us, but they did
not know that we were seeds.

~ Mexican Proverb

Karen and I found employment shortly after returning to Oregon following our hasty departure from Haiti. Sher'ri finished high school and joined her sister Shela among the young adults known as college students. We settled into a steady rhythm of life in our home culture.

From time to time we heard reports from Haiti. We rejoiced that the chaos that led to destruction and theft in Port-au-Prince never migrated to Dessalines. The hospital in Dessalines had a standard door with a simple lock in the doorknob. Even though someone could have easily kicked in the door, no one disturbed the hundreds of thousands of dollars worth of equipment and supplies. The five apartments had been furnished, even with dishes in the kitchen cabinets. Everything remained as it was when I left Dessalines on that Friday afternoon.

An opportunity came to us to assist a congregation in southern Mexico, near the border with Guatemala. We almost said no to the request, but we eventually agreed to lead a team of twenty-three people.

On our last evening in Mexico, the pastor came to visit at the hotel where we stayed. He surprised us by dumping a pile of jewelry on the table in the center of our group: gold watches, rings, bracelets, and necklaces. He told us that he recently talked to his congregation about the cost of constructing a new church building. He told the people that they would never be able to reach their goal through offerings; the people's meager income would not allow it. He challenged the people to find creative ways to help the congregation move toward its goal. That day when they received the tithes and offerings, people removed jewelry and placed it in the offering plates.

The pastor pointed out that each piece of jewelry on the table in front of us had a small tag on which was written the value if sold to a jewelry store. Karen selected a small gold chain for her wrist. She wore it every day for eighteen months, a prompt to pray for her friends in Mexico. Only months later did I learn that Karen also used that gold chain as a reminder of her commitment to God to spend nothing on herself so she could give more to others. No new dress, no new shoes.

God used the commitment of our Mexican friends to deepen our own transformation as Christ followers. We saw God working in remarkable ways on that trip, and we began to envision our involvement with people who did not speak Creole. We realized that we had so fixated on one place, one culture, one skin color, that we had not considered other options. If the political circumstances in Haiti made our return impossible, we could find other places of service.

We started a cycle of working in Oregon to support a short-term mission trip. We worked just long enough to pay for the next trip of eight weeks or five months. I knew with my construction skills I could always get a job, so that freed us to consider multiple invitations. During those years we assisted in Mexico (two teams), Haiti (three teams), Swaziland (three teams), Kenya, Venezuela (three teams), and Brazil (one team with forty-two people).

Our main project in Swaziland was about three hundred yards from a mission hospital. The doctor invited me to spend one day with him watching the surgeries. One operation involved a man who had been speared. Without diagnostic imagining machines, the doctor did exploratory surgery in which he discovered that the spear entered the man's body in an armpit, missed vital organs, but ruptured his colon. The doctor reversed the colostomy on the day I observed. I watched with amazement as the doctor stitched the slippery and floppy tissue back together. From time to time, the doctor stepped back from the operating table, rolled his shoulders, shook off the muscle tension, and returned to stitching.

A nurse called the doctor just about the time he finished the surgery. A man arrived at the hospital after being shot in the back with a shotgun. The doctor attended to this man while he lay on a gurney in the hallway. The next operation involved a mastectomy because of breast cancer. I marveled at how the doctor carefully removed cancerous tissue, and then stretched the skin to close the extensive incision.

Throughout my life, I often donated blood at a mission hospital. Friends from our congregation in the United States came to work with us in Swaziland and they, too, donated blood. One friend had a rare blood type. The lab technician called out the blood type just as a doctor walked through the room. The doctor stopped and asked the lab tech to repeat the blood type. A newborn needed one-quarter unit of that blood type to survive. The right type at the right time. We rejoiced.

In December 1990, I received a telephone call with an urgent request that we go to Kenya to manage the construction of Africa Nazarene University (ANU). Eight short-term mission teams had already committed to making the trip in 1991 and a personnel change left the project in need of a superintendent. I explained that we had just returned from Swaziland. I had two construction projects lined up and Karen had started a new job that would help us replenish our bank account. I told the caller that we were not in the financial position to take another assignment at that time. When outside financial assistance came through, however, I boarded an airplane for Kenya. Karen gave notice to her new employer and flew to Nairobi with the second team to assist with the ANU project that year.

Twenty-five African workers made up the construction crew. University students worked on weekends to help build their campus. Until we arrived, the workers, students, and short-term mission team members mostly kept to themselves. We started bringing the groups together for meals and required that they alternate in the food line: African, American, African, American. That simple step broke down barriers and caused people to begin talking to one another. Toward the end of the eleven months we spent at ANU, one African worker told me, "Since you came to Kenya, I have lost my fear of white people." I rejoiced to hear that testimony.

Once again, a way opened and we went. At first we did not see a financially feasible way to respond to the invitation, but things worked out as we took step after step. We faced obstacles, opposition that at times felt insurmountable, but we kept moving.

By this point in our lives, Karen and I eagerly looked forward to the next opportunity. We wanted to make another international trip to assist in a building project of some type. But we realized that we needed to make some changes in how we financed our work.

Ray, the associate pastor who designated me as the project leader on my first international trip, invited me to join him for lunch soon after we returned from Honduras. I thought it a bit strange when he counseled me to limit our debt. "If someday God called you and Karen to be missionaries," he said, "you will want the option to say yes. If you have too much debt, you will not be able to say yes even if you wanted to." We followed his advice, not because at the time we envisioned ourselves as living overseas, but it just made sense to us. So debt did not pose a problem for us.

Linda, the friend who assisted with preparing our income taxes, expressed concern about our lack of financial sustainability. "I know your earnings for the year," she told us, "and I know how much you give away. If you don't change the way you operate, some day you will be a financial burden to your daughters."

As the pull increased toward another long-term ministry assignment, Karen and I began to explore creating a nonprofit organization. We invited Ray, Linda, and my brother, Floyd, to meet us for breakfast. We talked about who might contribute to further the mission that had gained clarity in our thinking. We discussed the legal process of starting a 501(c)3 qualified agency. Our three friends pledged to be involved in the new adventure and the five of us became the initial board of directors for GAP International.

The name selected for the organization reflected the type of work we had done and that which we expected to continue doing in the future. Karen and I filled the gap; we provided expertise that many mission agencies did not have among their existing personnel. As self-funded volunteers, we could expand the capacity for ministry without being a financial drag on the mission agency. We wanted to collaborate and to do so without being a burden.

I left the breakfast meeting with the realization that we had started a new chapter in our lives. We just needed to work through all of the organizational details.

I received a telephone call about twelve hours after the breakfast meeting. "You may not remember me," the man said. "I am Dean from Chicago."

Of course I remembered Dean. He had been on a short-term mission team that came to work at Africa Nazarene University. Dean and I worked side by side for several days. He asked a lot of questions as we worked, about my motivation to live and work in Kenya, about my family in the United States. One evening after dinner, Dean told the story of a terrible accident. Dean and his wife stopped by their new house under construction. His wife wanted to take a photo and she asked Dean to back up a bit so she could better frame the picture. Dean unknowingly stepped over the edge and fell into the basement. Dean broke his back. The infant son he held in his arms had a serious head injury. The ambulance workers who responded to the 911 call did not have the necessary equipment to get Dean and the infant out of the basement; the builders had yet to install the stairs.

As I listened to Dean tell this tragic story, I tried to imagine what he must have thought while laying on the concrete floor. I wondered about his wife; she must have been frantic as she waited for help. I remembered my own experience of lying on concrete, broken.

As Dean continued his story, he became quite emotional as he talked about their friends in the old neighborhood. "They were like Christ in every way," he said. "Our loving neighbors introduced us to a loving God."

Yes, I remembered Dean. I had thought of this story several times in the year since I first heard it.

"Swanee," Dean said, "I received a bonus at work and I want you to find a way to use it. And I mentioned this to a co-worker and he wanted to join me. So I'd like to send you a check for fifty-five hundred dollars." I smiled at the timing of Dean's telephone call.

I told Dean about the breakfast meeting earlier in the day. I said that his telephone call confirmed the action we had taken that morning. I told Dean that we needed to get organized and I would be back in touch. Several weeks later we opened a bank account for GAP International with a deposit of fifty-five hundred dollars.

I started exchanging e-mails with the Oregon representative of World Gospel Mission (WGM). I told him of our skills and our availability to move to Africa if we might contribute to WGM's ministry there. The Oregon man sent an introduction of us to the WGM director in Kenya. I inadvertently received a copy of the reply; "Do not let this couple get away. We have been looking for someone just like them." At this point I knew enough about the situation in Kenya that I could tell we could play a strategic role with World Gospel Mission. They did not want us to come just because we provided our own support through the partners of GAP International. We could fill a need by just being ourselves. We soon finalized the arrangements.

As we prepared to move to Kenya, I created a list of tools and equipment I would eventually load into a sea-land container. I started looking at classified ads in the newspaper. One day I left work to see a trailer that sounded just like what I needed. When I pulled up to the address I had been given, I could tell that the trailer behind the red and white for sale sign could not endure Kenyan roads. The owner came bounding out the door, so I explained that I needed a different type of trailer than what he had for sale.

"Why won't it work for you?" he demanded.

"I'm shipping it to Africa," I replied, describing the type of materials and tools I would haul with the trailer.

"Do you need any tools?" The man continued talking even as I tried to move toward my truck. This stranger was eating up my time; I wanted to get back to work. He insisted that I see his tools.

As I entered the backyard, I saw a workshop and several smaller toolsheds. This man had a lot of tools. I found out that he retired as a heating, ventilation, and air conditioning contractor. As he took me from place to place in the backyard, he asked questions about our work in Haiti and what I would be doing in Africa. After he listened to my answers, he surprised me by offering to give me any of the tools or building materials I could use in Africa. I was stunned at the generosity.

When I arrived the next day with a trailer to pick up the tools, the man's story began to tumble out. As a young man, this retired contractor wanted to be a missionary. Living in another country was not an option after he married and had a family. He kept talking as we loaded the trailer: Lincoln welder, Ridgid pipe vise, pipe wrenches, pipe cutters, saws, drills, grinders, hand tools, aluminum ladder with the company name painted on the side in forest green paint, electric hammer drill, several extension cords, rolls of new electrical wire, rolls of copper tubing. I accepted only tools and materials I knew I would use. After ninety minutes, I tied the load to the trailer, thanked my new friend for his generosity, and got in the pickup to leave. As I sat in the driver's seat, my friend stood at the open window, weeping. "I am happy to know that my tools are going to Africa," he said. "I'll never get to go myself, but I can't thank you enough for taking my tools with you."

Hundreds of times in the next seven years I picked up a tool or climbed a ladder painted forest green and remembered a man I met through a classified ad for a trailer inadequate for my use but who still became a partner. The way opened and I had companions for the journey.

Chapter 13

Seven Days

Having conversation is like having riches.

~ Kenyan Proverb

Karen and I lived in Kenya seven years, but we never could have survived even seven weeks if the schedule would have been anything like the first seven days! On the day we arrived in Kenya in 1994 we could not have predicted the travel still to come that same week. The suitcase had a few more adventures in the days ahead that we did not anticipate when we left Oregon.

When moving halfway around the world, the transition starts days before boarding the airplane. Prior to this move to Kenya, we emptied our house and turned it over to a real estate management agency to find someone who would pay us to live there. We were already tired as we boarded the plane in Portland. After about sixteen hours we landed in London. We boarded another plane several hours later for the eight-hour flight to Nairobi. Our body clocks were out of whack as we searched for our suitcases in customs, the sum of busy preparations, a long travel itinerary, and the ten hour difference in time zones.

We rejoiced when we walked out of the immigration and customs area and saw a man holding a sign that simply read, "WGM." World Gospel Mission, the agency we worked with for seven years in Kenya and three years in Uganda, sent a driver to take us to the guest house.

We had previously stayed at this guest house. Located in a residential area, it provided a quiet place to rest. Coming through the gate, we saw numerous cars, some with blue plastic tarps covering them. Missionaries left cars at this guest house while they were out of the country. At night the guard dog roamed freely in the compound.

Our room was upstairs, one of three guest rooms. The room was so small that you could not leave a suitcase opened on the floor. A simple pull down shade covered the window. Bath towels were small. All guests shared one bathroom.

If you informed the guest-house personnel in advance, they provided meals. For breakfast we had eggs prepared to order, toast, and Kenyan tea. After a restful night and a good breakfast, we were ready for the beginning of the new chapter of living in Kenya.

We knew that the Nairobi Central Church of the Nazarene was close by, so we walked from the guest house to the church. To our great surprise, at the church we found friends then living in Ethiopia. "What brings you back to Kenya?" I asked after we greeted each other.

"We're here to sell our vehicle," came the reply.

"We need to purchase a car," I said. "What do you have?" It turns out that I knew about the particular four-wheel drive vehicle they had for sale from when we previously lived in Kenya for eleven months. It was about four years old. Since I knew who had driven it, I felt confident that we would not be surprised to discover a hidden problem.

"We leave for the airport in thirty minutes," our friend said, "and the car is clear on the other side of the city. If you think you might want it, give me a personal check and I'll sign the title today. After you see the vehicle tomorrow, if you don't want it, call me in Ethiopia and I'll tear up the check. If you do wish to buy it, I'll cash your check next week." He told us the vehicle had been appraised at twenty-two thousand dollars, and lowest he could go was seventeen thousand dollars.

I immediately recognized God had been at work. During our last few days of packing, we received a phone call from the mission director in Kenya. He told us of his excitement to have us join their team. He said they were praying for us. He asked about how the fundraising had gone. When I told him that we had seven thousand dollars toward the purchase of a vehicle, he replied, "What you can buy for seven thousand dollars will require constant repairs. You really need to double that amount." When we ended that conversation I was not sure what we would do.

On the last afternoon at our house in Oregon, just as we were ready to lock and leave, we received a phone call from a woman who wanted to see us immediately.

"You don't know me," she said, "but I know about you through my son who is in a Bible study group with your son-in-law, Gary. I want to come by in about thirty minutes to visit with you."

For days we packed and cleaned. Finally we were ready to close the door and drive away. I was not ready to chitchat with a stranger.

"This really isn't a good time," I said. "We have no furniture to welcome you. We are just now leaving our home and we fly to Africa tomorrow."

She came anyway.

We listened carefully as she told us about her mother who had recently died. Her husband was unfaithful. She had an adult son who struggled with a terminal illness. Each story she told became a crashing wave of emotion, pounding her again and again. She apologized for taking our time, but then launched into another story. We wept together. We prayed for God to comfort her.

Near to the end of an hour, she said, "My mother left me some money. I thought about giving it to the college where my brother is the president, but the school is so big I'm sure they will not even recognize my contribution." As she spoke, she started writing a check.

The next morning, on our way to the airport, we deposited a check for ten thousand dollars. Once again God's blessing came at what seemed to us to be an inconvenient time.

When we arrived in Kenya we had the seventeen thousand dollars already in the checking account to purchase the vehicle we would drive for the next seven years. God ordered a series of events on two continents that revealed God's gracious care and provision.

When we finally found a ride across Nairobi to the World Gospel Mission office, they implied we were an answer to their prayers. I do not recall if they asked us or told us, but they had decided we would deliver a new ambulance to Tenwek Hospital. A Christian organization provided the ambulance and it sat outside the office just waiting for us to take it on the five-hour trip to Bomet. I didn't even know which road to take to get out of Nairobi.

We had enough experience with various mission agencies to know that you did what you needed to do when you heard it needed to be done. Sometimes being a missionary is like signing a blank check. Someone else will fill in the amount and the date. We never would have imagined saying "no" to a request to drive an ambulance. Besides, they said we were an answer to their prayers. You can't argue with God at a time like that.

So the next morning we tossed a suitcase into the back, climbed into the ambulance, and headed northwest out of Nairobi toward Tenwek Hospital. This ambulance was a four-wheel-drive Land Cruiser, a heavy-duty vehicle necessary for reliable service on tough Kenyan roads. In Kenya, an ambulance is used only for transportation. They do not have medical equipment nor provide medical care while transporting a patient. On this occasion, the ambulance was packed floor to ceiling—overloaded, in fact—with boxes of Bibles to be delivered to the missionaries.

Remember, just a few days prior I drove my car in Oregon. Now I'm a jet-lagged driver in Kenya where the steering wheel is on the right side of the car. In my head I'm driving an ambulance on the "wrong" side of the road in Nairobi. Animals and children and motorcyclists play chicken with the weaving traffic in Kenya. So what is the logical thing to do in a situation like that? Okay, I admit that sometimes I enjoyed turning on the siren to clear the road ahead of us. That kept Karen awake, too.

As we prepared to leave to deliver the ambulance, a thoughtful office worker handed us a half-sheet of paper, less a map and more a list of directions. Take the highway until you come to the Rift Valley. Pass through Nakuru. Turn left towards Lake Victoria. We did okay until the instructions said to turn left when leaving Kericho. We started driving through tea fields and wondered if we had made a wrong turn, but we continued until it became a two-lane gravel road. After driving on this road for about an hour, we turned around. We eventually discovered that instead of making a left turn, we should have just stayed on the left side of the "Y" when the road split.

We finally made it. The crazy Americans with no clue about the road to their destination delivered the ambulance only two hours late. The folks at Tenwek Hospital provided meals and a place to sleep for the night.

The next morning a small airplane buzzed the Tenwek Hospital. That served as the announcement that the Mission Aviation Fellowship plane was on the final approach. A driver took us to the dirt airstrip about three miles from the hospital for our flight to Nairobi.

My first task when back in Nairobi involved getting new tires for the 4×4 vehicle that I purchased sight unseen. Once the vehicle had four new tires, we loaded our luggage and were on our way.

Our first destination was to pick up friends. We had yet to settle in as residents of Kenya when our first visitors arrived. We had met Phil and Pat previously while working at the Africa Nazarene University campus. They were teachers from Chicago who loved to work on short-term mission projects. Our last meeting had been in 1992 while we were working in Venezuela. Since Phil and Pat had been in Tanzania and knew of our new ministry in Kenya, they arranged to go home through Nairobi to be with us a few days.

So on day five of our first week in Kenya, Phil and Pat agreed to help us take our "new" 4×4 upcountry where we would live for the next several years. We headed for Kericho, the city that would be our new hometown. Laughter filled our time as we retraced the journey Karen and I had taken in the ambulance just two days before.

About two hours before reaching Kericho, we stopped to see Dean and Leta, the couple who led the ministry of World Gospel Mission in Kenya. Dean was the author of the e-mail that landed in my e-mail box by accident and the one who told me that I needed to double the amount I planned to spend on a vehicle. I eagerly wanted him to see the vehicle God provided.

We arrived at Dean and Leta's house in the late afternoon and soon sat down at their table for dinner. They answered numerous questions about their experiences living in Kenya. Leta talked about the foods and seasonings available, and we learned how to make a pseudo apple pie with what could be purchased at a Kenyan market. This was the beginning of a wonderful relationship.

Toward the end of the meal, Dean asked a question that I suspect had been percolating for a while. "Once a month I drive about nine hours north," he said, "to deliver dry beans, rice, oil, and kerosene to a single missionary. Would you and Phil like to ride along with me tomorrow?"

Before going to sleep that night, I had my toothbrush and a change of clothes ready to go.

Even before sunrise on my sixth day in Kenya, Dean, Phil, and I headed down the road. We were going to the Kerio Valley and the remote village of Ng'rong. Dean drove a red Land Rover, a vehicle owned by a doctor at Tenwek Hospital. Before the end of the day, I learned that only the most robust of vehicles could make this trip.

As we traveled, Dean told one story after another. In the process he taught me how to live in East Africa.

We headed for an area where the Pokot people lived among thorn trees and bushes. These nomadic people managed to survive by moving from place to place with their livestock: cows, camels, and goats.

Dean interrupted his own story to mention that the Pokot will sometimes wrap up in a blanket and sleep on the paved road because of the warmth that radiates from the tarmac. He said that it is essential to watch for dark colored bumps on the road as it might be a person sleeping with a few goats.

Dean began to explain in detail how WGM became involved planting churches in such a remote area with a challenging group of people. From the beginning this missionary effort was an act of great faith by a few people.

The first two Christians in the Kerio Valley came from the Pokot tribe. Two men gave up the typical Pokot occupation of grazing animals that often included stealing animals from other tribes. These two men traveled to another tribal area to work on the construction of the Turkwel hydroelectric dam. World Gospel Mission sent an African missionary to the Turkana people where the two Pokots heard the gospel and believed in Jesus as their Savior. When these men returned to their families, they asked WGM to send a missionary to teach them more about their new life in Christ.

I was learning so much as we drove that day.

Dean told me that African church leaders and missionaries opposed sending a pastor to the Pokot people. The Pokots had a reputation as being a challenging tribe with whom to work. Even the Kenyan government struggled to appropriately administrate the region. No other Christian church had established a ministry among the Pokots where David lived. The church leaders recognized the high risk of failure if they were to send a missionary to the Kerio Valley.

Dean told me about David volunteering to plant churches while still a Bible college student. As David approached graduation, many times he asked the church leadership to send him to the Pokot people. Dean finally tipped the conversation when he volunteered to personally visit David once a month. The church leaders and missionaries allowed Dean to "cosign" with David, and a pioneer mission was born.

The scenery changed as our journey continued. Dean said that the only regular transportation through the Kerio Valley was a truck that went through twice a week.

We came to a trading center, just a wide spot in the road with a cluster of stick and mud houses. We turned onto a rocky road, the beginning of the final eighteen miles. People from Ng'rong sometimes walked to the trading center. Or if they were lucky, people hitched a ride to the trading center on the "taxi" which was just a farm tractor pulling a large, heavy-duty, two-wheeled trailer. They rode the taxi at their own risk.

We drove on sand when we crossed a dry riverbed. The farther we drove, the more I began to feel how far removed we were from anything familiar. Few people from the outside will ever see Ng'rong.

I came to realize that seeking to minister to the Pokot people involved a huge commitment. The church leaders were correct; this was a challenging assignment that required great commitment and courage. The faith of Dean and David began to shine against that backdrop.

When David saw us drive up, he hurried to put on a shirt before coming to greet us. He had not known we were coming, but he obviously was delighted to see us. We quickly became the center of attention as several Pokot men gathered to shake hands with the three men from the United States. Some of the men were dressed like David with flip-flop sandals and short pants. Other men wore only a piece of cloth the size of a large tablecloth slung over one shoulder.

One man outside of the immediate circle stood bare naked, wearing only flip-flops. I later asked David about this man. "Most days he does cover himself," David replied, "but today being naked was no problem." David went on to explain that a Pokot man will go to great lengths not to expose his buttocks to a woman. He will even back up and put his butt against a wall or tree until the woman passes by.

As we stood talking in front of the ten-by-ten-foot metal building that David used as a house, in almost one motion David bent over, grabbed the back leg of a goat, picked it up, and walked eight feet to a tree perhaps twelve feet tall. David forced the goat's head into a fork formed by tree limbs. The small horns held it securely in place. David rejoined the circle of men as the conversation continued, a mixture of Pokot, English, and Kiswahili.

The poor goat yelled for help, but no one seemed to pay attention to what was happening just eight feet away. I quietly said to Phil, "I think we are going to eat goat tonight." He gave me a slight smile and nodded his head.

Just think, a few days prior Karen and I were in London, waiting for our next flight, and eating fast food at the airport. Now I was about to witness fast food Pokot-style. The London airport is constructed with steel and glass. I stood near houses built with sticks and mud. Travelers hurrying through the airport wore the latest fashions and carried personal items in designer bags. Now I was surrounded by Pokot men holding long spears and bows and arrows.

Perhaps ten minutes went by before David excused himself, took a few steps into his house, and came out with a sharp kitchen knife. Yes, we did have goat meat for dinner. One half was boiled and the other half was roasted over a fire. I love roasted goat meat! As the meat cooked, I said to David, "I'm sure you have used that fork in the tree before."

His reply came immediately. "Yes, this is goat number twenty-eight since moving here two years ago."

Weather in the Kerio Valley can be very hot each day but by midnight it is down to seventy degrees, perfect for sleeping. Phil and I had pitched a tent. Dean opted to sleep on the floor of the Land Rover. David only used his house for sleeping and as a place to keep his few belongings out of the scorching sun.

After Dean and Phil were asleep, David and I sat in two straight-back chairs under a billion stars. Occasionally we heard murmurs from nearby people. Some goats and camels had bells tied on their necks, so we might hear a soft jingle. But mostly we sat together in the quiet darkness.

I asked questions, important questions. David answered from the heart. He freely expressed his feelings about being alone. A big part of his loneliness came from the lack of meaningful conversation. "No one here knows about church history or theology," he told me. "No one here can discuss politics or books or even talk about the rest of Kenya. The men mostly talk about AK-47 guns, camels, goats, and stealing animals near the bridge at Tot. That's about it. No one knows or cares to know what I know." For two years David had longed for meaningful conversation in English. My heart went out to him.

David told me, "Sometimes all I can do is laugh because nothing seems to change around here." So as the conversation jumped from subject to subject, I looked for ways to make David laugh. We laughed at silly things. There we were in this remote village among the Pokot people, the two of us sitting on straight-back chairs under a dark canopy with twinkling stars, talking and laughing.

I went to sleep sometime after one o'clock that night.

As the sun rose later that morning, we climbed into the Land Rover for the trip back to Nakuru. Dean started describing how David and seventy people gathered under shade trees down by the dry riverbed for worship services. Someday David would marry and would need a house for his family to live in: stone walls, metal roofing, glass windows, and two secure doors. He would need a bench on the front porch so visitors could have a comfortable place to sit and talk.

"Can you build a house for David?"

Before I could reply, Dean added, "Can you come back the next year to build the first church in the Kerio Valley?"

I did not know how to even begin to formulate a response. This was just my seventh day in Kenya. Each day I had gone to a different place, each night I slept in a different bed. *How could I build a house in Ng'rong when I did not even know where I would live in Kericho? What would Karen think? How could I get bags of cement and lumber and window glass delivered to this remote location? Who would pay for these building materials?* So many questions came to mind.

The only thing I knew for sure was that my 4×4 vehicle with new tires and a heavy duty Warn winch on the front could easily handle the roads, even while pulling the tandem-axle trailer that at the moment was somewhere in a sea-land container on its way to East Africa. We had not planned in advance the purchase of this 4×4, but taking advantage of the opportunities as they opened at least made it possible to say yes to the kind of appeal I just heard.

But I still needed to unpack my suitcases and get settled. "What if I say no?" I asked Dean.

Dean's reply was truthful and to the point. "Leta and I will soon retire. WGM has no one to oversee building projects. If you cannot do this, it just won't be done."

Dean looked straight ahead as we bounced along the rutted roadway.

"That's okay," he continued, "I'm not pressuring you to say yes. I'm just being honest."

I like straight talk.

Chapter 14

Beginnings

The grass suffers when elephants fight.

~ Kenyan Proverb

When Karen and I moved to Kenya, we used the Kenya Highlands Bible College in Kericho as our home base. The first place we called home was a small, one-bedroom house on the college campus. We moved in with only our suitcases while we waited for the sea-land shipping container to arrive.

I began to help with building repairs on the college campus using whatever tools the school owned. The college employed one man to do building maintenance and he was clearly over-worked and undertrained.

On one of the first days, I took a shortcut from my home to the workshop. About midway down the hill, I hopped over a broken down fence into tall grass. The tall grass prevented me from seeing a piece of wood with the nails sticking up. A big rusty nail went through my tennis shoe and deep into the arch of my foot. I hobbled the rest of the way down the hill. Once inside the workshop I sat down to check my foot and found my sock already red with blood. I needed help.

A missionary told me how to find a medical doctor in downtown Kericho. The doctor looked at my foot and said I needed a tetanus shot. There are too many risks with a rusty nail in a field that formerly served as a cattle pen. Since he did not have the necessary medicine in the office, he sent me to the pharmacist to buy tetanus serum and a syringe. I followed the doctor's directions, found the location, and hobbled into the pharmacy. I lucked out; what I needed was in stock.

As the pharmacist went to get the medicine, I looked around the store. This man had a well-organized pharmacy. While he was gone, I decided to play a joke on this guy. When he laid the serum and syringe on the countertop, I said, "The doctor only needs the vaccine. He already has a good supply of used needles."

This man almost jumped over the counter. I knew that healthcare workers sometimes used syringes again and again. The pharmacist knew that too and it caused him to get excited. Too excited! Even after I explained to him that what I said regarding the used syringe was only a joke, he kept warning me. He begged me not to let the doctor inject me with an old syringe. As I walked away with the new syringe and serum, I am sure the pharmacist still worried for my safety.

This interaction with the pharmacist became my first with those of Indian descent living in Kericho, many of whom observed the Hindu religion. Within a few weeks of arriving in Kericho, Karen and I had moved out of our transitional housing on the Bible college campus. We found only one good option, a five-unit apartment building in the town of Kericho. Indians occupied the other four apartments. Three families were in business and our next-door neighbor was a medical doctor.

While riding in my car one day, a prominent church leader asked what I considered a strange question. After he called one of my neighbors by name, he said, "Is that man your best friend?"

It felt like a confrontational question to me, like somehow I had committed a sin, so I tried to deflect it. "I don't know if he is my *best* friend," I said, "but I do like him."

The church leader asked a second question. "When you are in his home, what do you talk about?"

This time I answered in a straightforward manner. "You can see that he has a big satellite dish on the outside of his house. Sometimes we watch CNN together." I paused as I considered what else I might say. "Sometimes he tells me about his teenage son," I continued. "He's very worried about his boy, and because I'm a bit older, I suppose, he asks for my advice."

The church leader listened quietly. In light of how I felt about being asked these questions, I took that as a good sign.

"I do not know why he does this, but sometimes he will talk about his frustrations with being a business owner in Kenya. And Karen is a good friend with three of the Indian women who live in our apartment building. They talk about things so personal that Karen will not even tell me about their frustrations." I am not sure my response satisfied the church leader.

As we settled into life in Kericho, I quickly realized that I needed a heavy-duty luggage rack on top of the 4×4 to carry suitcases and building materials. Because my tools had yet to arrive, I went to the only machine shop in Kericho to get a quote. The business owner gave me a price four times higher than I expected. I thanked him for the quote and went to the local hardware store for steel, paint, and a hand-held grinder. I cut the steel with a hacksaw and found a welding machine available to me. I used my new grinder to smooth the welds before I painted it.

I felt a bit nervous the next time I went to the machine shop. I wondered if I had destroyed any chance of having a good relationship with the owner. To my surprise, the opposite happened. This man looked at my luggage rack and declared that I had done an excellent job.

Over the next seven years we became good friends with this man and his family. They observed the Sikh religion. At least ten times our families shared a meal, usually at their home because this man lived with his wife, three children, his mother, and two sisters. I thought my rejection of his bid to build the roof rack might close the door. Our common commitment to quality work proved to be enough to initiate a lasting relationship.

We lived on the Bible college campus when we heard about a new restaurant in Kericho, so we made it a point to visit for a meal. Karen and I ate at this restaurant many times through the years. Sometimes we took friends with us. One time the Muslim family that ran the restaurant invited a work team of twenty persons to their home for a wonderful meal. The invitations went the other direction, too. The Muslim family came to our house. Because we lived within walking distance, the daughters came to visit Auntie Karen on occasion. Several years later, when we lived in Uganda, the oldest daughter said she wanted to visit Auntie Karen before she left for college in Indonesia. We enjoyed her four-day visit before we put her on the bus for the eleven-hour ride back to Kenya.

So here we were, United States citizens living in Kericho, Kenya. We worked mostly with Christians on the construction of church buildings. But our friends included Hindus, Muslims, and Sikhs. Seven years after our arrival, on the last four evenings in Kericho we had dinner with two Hindu families, a Muslim family, and a Sikh family. We had our schedule for the final week set before any of the missionaries or church leaders issued an invitation. I grieve that some of our Christian friends looked on us with suspicion because we gave priority to eating with non-Christians.

As we prepared to move to Kenya in 1994, we put everything in a sea-land container. In addition to our personal items, this twenty-foot container held a twelve-foot construction trailer, two concrete mixers, a gasoline welder, an electric welder, and many other things. It was an extremely heavy load. A company picked up the container at our house in Oregon. After weeks of travel between various ports and depots, we finally heard that our container had arrived in Africa. The shipping company put it on a train for transport from the east coast of Kenya to Nairobi. While in Nairobi, a freight forwarder finally released it to a trucker. The trip from Nairobi to Kericho would take about five hours in a car, so we estimated delivery in a day or two. When that did not happen, we made many phone calls to Nairobi and finally concluded that the container was lost . . . or stolen. We were sick. The contents had a value of about twenty thousand dollars. Without the tools we likely would have to return to the United States and start the process again.

About noon on the fifth day we got a telephone call. One of the teachers at the Bible college said that the container had arrived, but the driver had driven into a retaining wall. He damaged the truck and the wall. In a panic, the driver left with our container still on his truck.

Karen and I jumped in our car to see if we could find this truck on the highway. We located it near a police checkpoint. The driver was completely out of his mind, so the officers concluded that the man was either using drugs or alcohol. The driver and the truck with our container still on board spent the night at the police station. The next day when the police released the driver, he still acted like he was under the influence of something.

Once he got near the Bible college, he started to turn the truck around, apparently afraid to go back to where he had the accident the day before. I asked if I could drive the truck.

"Absolutely not," he said. I later learned that thieves often stole trucks like this, so the driver had reason to reject my request.

I had to act quickly or risk losing the whole container. So I climbed onto the running board of this big truck and talked to the driver through the open window. I told him he was a good guy. I said that he could count on me to protect him. I assured him that I knew the people at the Bible college and that no one there would have him arrested.

As I stood on the running board, the driver slowly pushed the accelerator to begin the one-thousand-foot climb up the hill to the college campus. I noticed his hands were frozen on the steering wheel. He seemed paralyzed—fear, I suppose—as we approached the ninety-degree turn at the top of the hill. This was where he hit the wall the day before. Little by little, with the driver working the pedals and me tugging on the steering wheel, we made it around the corner. I breathed a sigh of relief when we finally made it down the other side of the hill where we would offload the container.

Because this occurred just before Christmas, only a few students remained on the campus. I hired these students to help unload the container. As quickly as possible, with the container still on the truck, we carried boxes and tools into a warehouse.

When we had unloaded everything but the two concrete mixers and the tandem-axle trailer, we decided to take a break. While Karen and I had refreshments with the students, we heard the truck engine start and drive away. I could not believe what I saw. The back doors of the container swung wildly with the equipment bouncing inside as he drove down the bumpy road.

Again, I raced ahead and got the Kenyan police to stop this crazy man at the roadblock. Again, they took the driver and the truck to the police station for the night. Again, I hurried back to the Bible college to find a padlock so I could lock up my container. The police suggested that it would be safe, but I knew better. Before I secured it for the night, I inspected the equipment. The trailer had fallen over and smashed into one of the mixers, but other than that, no damage done.

The next day, this time with a police escort, the driver brought the container to the campus for the third time. We unloaded the remaining tools with the use of a farm tractor. I felt great joy and relief as I watched this truck and driver leave the campus.

After he was gone, the students continued to help us as we separated tools from dishes and other personal items. We had both a workshop and a house to get organized.

While we worked, I looked to see the truck driver walking toward me. *He's back?!* The driver evidently prepared his speech while he walked. He told me that he knew he was a bad person and that he had trouble delivering the container because he had been drinking. Then he reminded me that it was near Christmas Day and asked if I would give him a bonus to make his trip back to Nairobi easier. He concluded his speech by reminding me that Jesus forgave people for their sins, and that I should forgive him and give him money.

I did not have to think about my response. "I am not Jesus," I said, "but I forgive you. I will not give you even one small coin. Now go."

The driver turned to walk back to wherever he had parked the truck.

Once my tools arrived, I could finally begin what I moved to Kenya to do. I drove about forty-five minutes from my home for a Sunday afternoon meeting with the pastor and congregational leaders for what became my first church project in Kenya. When I walked into this thirty-six-by-eighty-foot building, I saw at least a dozen small trees propping up the roof trusses. The most unusual sight, however, was that the church benches faced the back door, not the platform. The pastor quickly explained that the people wanted to face the exit in case the roof started to collapse during a service. "The building will have to come down," the pastor told me, "so we can rebuild."

They showed me cracks in the walls on both sides of the platform. The cracks did not look all that bad to me, but the ground obviously was shifting. I saw cracks in the floor on the platform. As we walked around the building, other persons commented that the building needed to come down. That seemed to have become the refrain repeated by all. I had yet to be convinced of the inevitability of tearing down the building, but I still needed to formulate an alternate solution, so I kept asking questions. This church used terrazzo flooring, an expensive and unusual material for a rural church. The sidewalls were nice with iron window frames and glass.

To buy myself a little more time, I continued my slow walk around the building. By the time my circuit brought me to the back of the building, a plan began to formulate in my mind. I invited the pastor and church leaders to sit with me inside the building. Even as I began to talk I was still working out the details in my mind.

What I proposed that day turned out to be exactly what we did. We removed the one-by-twelve-inch fascia board on both sides. That opened a way to insert new steel trusses between the top of the wall and the roof. Working on one truss at a time, we used seven car jacks to lift the roof so we could cut out a sagging wooden truss. With the jacks carrying the load, we welded the new steel truss in place. We removed the car jacks and moved to the next truss. It was a slow process, but we installed all of the trusses in five days. No one ever had to get on the roof; we completed all of the work from the inside.

I determined that the cracks in the floor and wall near the platform were the result of that end of the building resting on fill dirt. The building was at least twenty-five years old, so it was understandable that some settling had occurred. We added two rooms just outside of the existing building, one on each side of the platform. This gave us an excuse to dig deep and pour a solid concrete foundation for the new rooms. I used a rotor hammer to drill into the existing building and drove rebar into these holes. When we poured the concrete pillars for the new rooms, we poured over the rebar protruding from the old building. The new pillars also supported the old building so it would no longer sink. The congregation finished the two rooms, my crew reinstalled the fascia boards, and the project was done.

On the last day of our work on this project, I noticed a big man of about sixty years sitting in the back of the church, crying. One of his legs had been amputated at the knee. I quietly asked the pastor to tell me about this old man. The pastor said that this man served as the contractor for the original building. He was heartbroken when he heard the talk about taking down this building. He wept to know that his own work was not in vain. For a fraction of the cost of new construction, the congregation ended up with a larger, stable building.

That project began my church construction work in Kenya. Word spread quickly to the eight hundred congregations in the Africa Gospel Church. When I arrived in Kenya, one hundred fifty congregations had construction projects in the works. Knowing that I could not help all of the congregations, we formulated a plan that allowed me to concentrate our efforts on helping congregations get a good start on the construction before I brought in my crew to install the roof.

Chapter 15

Pokots in Ng'rong

A patient person will eat ripe fruit.
~ Kenyan Proverb

On the trip to Ng'rong the first week I was in Kenya, when Dean asked me to build a house for David and the first church in the area, I could not have predicted that over the next two and a half years I would spend seventeen weeks in the Kerio Valley. That initial trip provided almost all of my orientation to the region. Dean returned with us only one more time, to help us find stones to use in building. Other than that, I was on my own. I soon discovered that I had a lot to learn.

A typical trip from Kericho to Ng'rong was never typical. Something unexpected always seemed to occur. We would spend eleven hours on the road. We drove on paved roads for the first part of the trip, but without road signs or guardrails. Once we passed through Nakuru we saw houses, farms, schools, and small businesses. About two hours north of Nakuru we topped off the tanks at a small gas station. The gas tank on the 4×4 would hold enough to get us back to this spot on the way home, but we carried extra gas cans just in case.

When we turned off of the main road we started seeing cactus plants, some up to fifteen feet tall. Sometimes we stopped to take photos of the beautiful pink blossoms.

We began to see Pokot people when we came to the trading center. We recognized them by the traditional Pokot clothing: women in cow skin skirts and men with a large cloth draped over one shoulder. We often bought cold sodas at the trading center, our last chance for this type of treat since the electric grid ended there.

We often stopped for lunch along a dry riverbed. Under shade trees, we enjoyed our sandwiches and potato chips, fruit and carrot sticks. Since this rest stop had no facilities, each person would find a tree. I checked the ropes on the trailer and luggage rack before continuing the journey. The most difficult part of the trip lay ahead.

No sign indicated where to turn to go to Ng'rong. That was one of those things that you just had to know. Once down in the valley we began to see camel herds. The herders were there, guarding their prized possessions, but seldom could you see them from the car.

Crossing a dry riverbed posed a challenge since we could quite easily get stuck in the sand. Pulling a trailer loaded with building materials increased the danger—bags of cement, wood for roof trusses, iron window frames, steel doors, roofing, paint, welding rods, padlocks, glass and glazing putty, metal legs and wood for church benches, and all of the tools we needed to do the job. Stopping in the middle of the riverbed or even shifting gears resulted in terrible consequences.

Deep ruts ran through the roadway. With the 4×4 and trailer stretched out, one end could be coming out of a rut just as the other end dropped. From the air we must have looked like the waves on the ocean. This slowed the progress considerably.

The rocks we drove over had sharp edges. These were not river rocks that had been smoothed and rounded. The rocky points beat up tires. You needed to watch for thorns, too. The three-inches thorns in the area could penetrate a tire, or a shoe. I always traveled with two spare tires for the 4×4 and one for the trailer. I kept a tire tube repair kit close at hand. I always preferred changing a tire on the two-axle trailer than the 4×4 since I could position the good tire of the trailer on a rock to lift the tire I needed to change. With the 4×4 I would have to use the jack.

We felt relief when we finally pulled in to Ng'rong after eleven hours in transit. Karen planned a dinner that could be easily prepared as we got settled for the first night.

We could only carry enough food and water for ten to twelve days, so that determined the length of our trips to Ng'rong. We needed one gallon of water per day per person. We packed three ice chests, some with frozen beef, chicken, and bacon. Karen often included a frozen cake or cinnamon rolls. Since we could not keep food frozen for ten days, meals toward the end of a trip tended to be more boring than those at the beginning.

Karen and I slept in a yellow canvas tent given to us by retiring missionaries. It was waterproof, but the zippers were difficult to work. We slept on wood-frame army cots. After dark, we put on a swimsuit and bathed with a bucket and cup.

The arid conditions made life difficult for the Pokot people. As a result, they became resourceful in finding ways to survive in the harsh environment.

One day I visited a man in his house. The sticks that formed the walls looked more like a fence that formed an eight-foot square. He did not have a door that closed, just an opening into the house. The only cover was a single sheet of metal roofing mounted directly over the bed. Four bedposts held the roofing, the posts at the head of the bed taller than those at the foot. A piece of gutter at the bottom channeled any rain that fell into a bucket. The bed was at least three feet off of the ground to allow room for the goats to sleep under the owner. The mattress was cowhide stretched on tree branches with a diameter the size of a broom handle.

Milk is a staple in the Pokot diet. Camel milk is pale yellow, thick and sticky. The consistency reminded me of Elmer's glue. The Pokot people think tea loaded with camel milk and honey is quite the treat.

Honey may be as much as twenty-five percent of the Pokot diet. They are great beekeepers. The Pokots cut lengthwise a log that is about a foot in diameter and three to four feet long, and then hollow it out. A beekeeper will wire the two pieces together and hang it high in a tree as a hive. The thorn bushes produce little white flowers that the bees use to make honey. Many times the Pokot gave us a gift of about sixteen ounces of honey, but we never ate it for two reasons: the honey had pieces of dead bee parts and I-don't-know-what-else, and the glass jar previously contained medicine they used to inject their cows. We never had confidence that our bodies could handle the honey, so we passed on the gift to our Kenyan workers who enjoyed it.

A wild fruit grows in the area that is poisonous until boiled all day. The women gather a handful of fruit, drop it in a pot of water, set the pot on three stones, and build a fire under it. After the pot boiled for several hours, they changed the water and brought it again to a boil. They repeated the cycle at least three times. I'm told that the end result has a sour taste, even when mixed with milk and blood.

Pokot men often had a spear or bow and arrows near at hand. They also carried poison with them, a black tar-like substance made in the Kerio Valley. They dip the arrowhead in the poison before shooting their victim. They told me that they could easily identify a person who had been poisoned since the body swells and begins to decompose quickly.

146

One day I put out the word that I wanted to buy a bow and some arrows. Very soon a man came to me with a long bow and five arrows. I turned the bow at various angles and inspected the arrows. I asked the man, "Does the bow shoot straight?" The owner took the bow, gently laid an arrow on the bowstring, quickly lifted the bow, and buried the arrowhead in a tree trunk twenty feet away. The accuracy astounded me given how swiftly he aimed and fired. I purchased the bow, but declined the vial of poison that was offered.

Pokot women often experience violence directed toward them. On one trip, I heard a commotion outside the tent early one morning. David told me that I needed to take a girl to the hospital. He explained that it would be on a road I did not know and that it would take about ninety minutes one way.

The fourteen-year-old girl came from a family that faithfully attended the church. She was not married, but became pregnant when working in the house of a middle-aged man who worked for the government. I went with David to see for myself what was going on. The young mother had gone into labor. One leg of the baby stuck out of the mother. They told me that this had been the case for several hours.

I removed the back seats of the 4×4 and laid a green plastic tarp on the floor. This would be the bed for the girl. Five others traveled with us that day. When we arrived at the small rural hospital, I was extremely thankful the girl was still alive. We left the girl in the care of the healthcare workers and retraced our steps to Ng'rong.

On another occasion, David and I distributed corn provided by the Kenyan government. About fifty women stood in line that day. One at a time, I poured two heaping gallon cans of corn into the goatskin bags the women held open and David recorded each woman's name. I noticed a woman about half-way back in line move about twenty feet away. Other women surrounded her. She grabbed a tree branch, squatted down, and delivered a healthy boy. Twenty minutes later she was back in line to get her corn.

Pokot women hold the key to the survival of the Pokot people. They build the houses, care for the children, and milk the goats and camels. Their hands are as rough and tough as a tree branch.

The women played an important role in the construction we accomplished in Ng'rong. In seventeen weeks we completed a four-room house for pastor David, a thirty-by-seventy-foot church building, and a sixteen-by-thirty-foot prefab church at a preaching point ten miles from our main projects. We could not have completed our work without the women.

We needed to remove several thorny trees from the site where the first church went up. The tree trunks had a diameter of about ten inches. An ax just bounced off of the tree. When David saw the men I brought with me struggling with the first tree, he suggested that we turn the task over to the women. I watched in amazement.

The women dug around the base of the tree until they exposed the roots. When they found an opening between two roots, they forced a five-foot railroad bar through the gap. Four skinny women pulled on the bar. They reset it, then pulled again. They laughed as they worked. Eventually a root snapped. They repeated the cycle all the way around the base of the tree. By lunch time the first tree lay on the ground, conquered by persistent women.

The women carried the water needed to mix the concrete. In the dry riverbed, about two hundred yards down the hill from the job site, they dug a hole until they were close enough to the water table that water began to seep in. Sometimes they dug down ten feet. When water began to puddle, they dipped and poured the water into a jerrycan. Using leather straps around the forehead or as a sling around the shoulders (like carrying a backpack), the women hauled the water up the hill to the fifty-five gallon drum that sat next to the gas-powered concrete mixer.

The women lugged the sand and gravel up the hill also. They laid a cow skin on the ground, filled it with sand or gravel, and folded the corners to form a package. Somehow they got the load up on their shoulders and walked to the job site.

David kept a logbook of who carried what. I bought corn at a wholesale warehouse in Nakuru that we used to compensate the women for their work.

On our first work trip to Ng'rong, David, Karen, and I had lunch together. The workers from David's congregation lay down under a tree for a nap while we ate. That bothered me, that we had food and my new friends did not. So on all other trips we brought with us fifty pounds of beans and one hundred pounds of rice. The first thing in the morning, the women gathered firewood, carried water, and began preparations for lunch. Mealtimes became an important opportunity for building relationships.

After lunch, I went back to work with the men who traveled with me. Karen met with the women workers for about a half hour. She discovered that the women had a lot of questions that went unanswered. Because of cultural norms they could not ask David these questions. Sometimes the women wondered about the Bible. Other times they asked questions about being a mother. One time Karen brought a book with charts that showed how the physical body functions.

After a while, the Pokot women shared deeply personal things with Karen. One afternoon a woman voiced a prayer request. "I know I should stop making my husband angry," she said, "but I keep doing it. Even when I know he will beat me, I still do it."

Through the translator, Karen asked, "What do you do that is so bad?"

"I take my time in preparing the food," she said. "And at night I leave his bow and arrow by the tree. I am supposed to bring it in, but I do not do it. That makes my husband angry."

After a while Karen began to see that the Pokot women were starved for attention. As we started watching closely, we realized that we never saw Pokot people touch each other. Mothers would not even lovingly cradle a baby or caress a young child. So Karen started giving hugs to the women. At first the women stiffened and stared straight ahead, but eventually they started to giggle with the hugs. On one trip, when our vehicles pulled into Ng'rong, a dozen women lined up shoulder to shoulder waiting for Karen to give them a hug.

David had started a preaching point about ten miles away. Women from that congregation walked to be with Karen also. It looked to us like they just wanted to be with other people. Christian companionship took on an increased importance for us as we watched the Pokot women gather for fellowship.

I also learned a lot by watching two Pokot men. They must have been close to sixty years old. The shorter man was blind. The taller man helped him get around as each held the end of a five-foot stick, the taller man walking in front. They worked as a team in the construction of their church building. The blind man shoveled sand or gravel into a wheelbarrow, his friend wheeled it to where we needed it, then returned the empty wheelbarrow to the blind man. I observed this partnership day after day.

One Sunday morning, I watched these two men kneel next to each other, praying together. I wept as I looked at those two men that morning. They lived in an environment far removed from where I lived. They ate food very different from what I preferred. I had financial resources available to me that they could not even dream of. But all of that faded in light of the richness of being brothers in Christ.

Chapter 16

Forty-four Hours

To get lost is to learn the way.
~ Kenyan Proverb

With just a bit more daylight remaining, we hurried to gather our things before darkness made the task more difficult. We had just finished work for the day and needed to put a few things away before dinner. When we pulled out the next morning, we would have completed our fifth trip to Ng'rong. I would finish loading the trailer after some sleep.

Karen cried out.

I hurried over to find her lying on the ground next to the tent. She moaned in pain. Her leg. She lay beside a large black plastic bag. We had started bringing used clothes with us to distribute to the women.

"I came around the corner of the tent and tripped," Karen told me. "I heard the bones pop."

I looked and could see an obvious break on her right leg just above the ankle. *Oh, my. What do we do now?*

By this time David stood next to me. We began to move Karen into the tent. Carefully, not wanting to cause more pain, we lifted her, eased her past the tent flap and onto the army cot.

"I was moving fast," she said. "The bag was awkward to handle." It probably weighed thirty pounds.

I went back outside to try to figure out what happened. I found the rope still taut between the stake and the tent. The dry, hard ground held firm. Karen must have caught her foot under the rope right where it tied to the steel stake. A wedged foot plus momentum equaled disaster.

This is where things seemed to shift into slow motion. Memories of what happened next are a little fuzzy. Karen usually fixed the meals. I do not remember who prepared dinner that night. Karen typically packed our personal items. As far as I know we made it home with everything. It was like I shifted to autopilot. I am not sure about all that happened between when we lay Karen on the cot and when I lay down to try to get some rest.

I realized early on that it would be twelve hours before we could even start the trip to Tenwek Hospital. The trip from Ng'rong to the paved road was difficult enough during the day. It would be impossible (and impassable) at night. A flat tire, a common occurrence, could make us easy prey for robbers. So we just had to wait for daylight.

We did not have pain medicines with us. I listened to Karen moan throughout the night.

I went through all kinds of mental gyrations as I lay on my cot. My body was quiet, but my mind was not.

What can I do to get Karen to the hospital as quickly as possible?

I think there are Pokot sleeping on the ground outside the tent. Our friends are staying close by.

How could it be—so strong one moment, totally helpless the next?

I found it nearly impossible to sleep. Being near the equator, we had twelve hours of darkness every night of the year. Sleep came in chunks; minutes, not hours.

Very early the next morning I finished packing the trailer: ice chests, water containers, tools, and gas cans.

I lowered the passenger seat as far as possible and filled the space in front of the seat with luggage so we could elevate Karen's broken leg. I used pillows and sleeping bags to make it as comfortable as I could.

Our Pokot friends stood in small groups and quietly watched. After we moved Karen to the car seat, I collapsed the tent and loaded it and the cots onto the trailer. I double-checked the ropes. No Pokot riders this time.

With the vehicle in four-wheel drive, I shifted into first gear and slowly engaged the clutch. We waved to our friends. No one cried, but you could see the concern and sadness on their faces.

We generally cinched the seat belts tight when traveling over deeply rutted roads. We grabbed the bars mounted above the doors in an attempt to reduce the bouncing. This day we cinched the seat belts, gripped the bars, and I drove slowly . . . very slowly.

The road near Ng'rong was rocky. When we came to a dry riverbed, I had no choice but to speed up when driving through soft sand. With the trailer, I needed to gain enough speed to carry us across the sand and up the steep incline on the other side. The trailer sometimes caught in the sand and jerked the 4×4. That is when Karen cried out in pain. I told her how sorry I was, then tried to think of a better way to navigate the next tough spot. This cycle repeated again and again.

Traveling in and out of the Kerio Valley always required taking a leap of faith. If we had car trouble that we could not fix, it might be two days before another vehicle passed by. Cell phones and roadside assistance did not exist in northern Kenya. Faith sometimes comes with risk, and I felt the full weight of that risk on the day that Karen lay in the seat beside me.

153

A sense of desolation can settle in when leaving Ng'rong. Karen and I could drive for two hours or more and not see another person. We might notice a few camels and goats or log beehives high in a big tree, so we suspected that people sat nearby. But we did not see them. On this day we spent somber but fervent hours trying to get to the main highway.

The last little bit coming out of the valley posed a challenge in the best of times. This was not our best day. The road went through a cutout in the mountain, but still had a steep incline. Rocks the size of softballs made up the roadway. We bounced and shuddered and wobbled as I drove in first gear, maybe five miles per hour. I looked straight ahead, not at Karen. I could hear her pain, even if all she did was catch her breath. I needed to find the best route where no option was optimal.

Twelve hours after leaving Ng'rong—twelve long hours without pain pills—we pulled up to the house of Dick and Leta in Nakuru. We could usually make the trip in nine hours, but I drove more cautiously that day to minimize how much Karen would be jostled. We left Ng'rong in darkness; we arrived in Nakuru in darkness. A long, long day.

Leta provided some pain medicine that gave Karen a little relief. We ate, and then lay down for some rest. It had been more than twenty-four hours since Karen broke her leg. We slept better this night.

The next morning we continued our journey toward the medical care Karen needed. I felt more hopeful after rest and a good breakfast provided by our friends. We arrived in Kericho after three more hours of driving. I disconnected the trailer. Just doing that made things easier. I carried Karen up the seventeen steps to our apartment. She took a sponge bath. I carried her back downstairs to the car for the final part of what may be one of the most difficult trips of our lives.

Ninety minutes later Karen sat in a wheelchair at Tenwek Hospital. After x-rays, the American surgeon put a walking cast on her broken leg. He made it extra heavy since he knew about Karen's high activity level.

Forty-four hours after Karen lay on the ground in Ng'rong, we left Tenwek Hospital. From the car we looked up at the large sign facing the roadway. The top line said "Tenwek Hospital." Under that it read, "We Treat, Jesus Heals." We had driven by that sign many times. On this day it had special meaning for these two tired followers of Jesus.

As I started to turn onto the highway that would take us home, I saw vehicles with flashing lights headed our way. In the lead were several black Mercedes with darkened windows. "That must be the president of Kenya," I told Karen. Then came at least ten more luxury vehicles, likely carrying high-level government officials and security officers. We witnessed a presidential motorcade.

"They must have closed the highway at least a half hour ago," I said, "to be sure the motorcade could travel freely. Just imagine the traffic congestion when the police remove the blockades. It will be a nightmare getting home."

About this time the last vehicle in the motorcade passed by. I looked to the left; no more cars. I looked to the right; I could see the flashing lights now almost a half mile away. Each flash seemed to mock me: flash, goodbye; flash, goodbye.

Why can't I be the last car? Someone has to be in last place. Who will know?

The race was on. I shifted gears like a race car driver as I tried to get closer to the motorcade. I was almost afraid to look at the speedometer.

Karen reached over to turn on our hazard lights.

I finally settled in about one hundred yards behind the last vehicle in the motorcade. Being in last place never felt so good. We sat tall in our seats as we waved at the screaming school children lining the roadway. They jumped up and down in glee as we whizzed past. Even adults at the local market stopped their shopping to watch the parade. Everyone wanted to catch a glimpse of the rich and powerful who lived in Nairobi. On this day they got to wave at a couple from Oregon, too.

We arrived in Kericho in just thirty minutes. I fought the urge to drive all the way to Nairobi; running with the big dogs released a huge shot of adrenaline. I almost forgot that I was the runt of the litter.

Shifting into lower gears, I made three turns and stopped directly in front of a large iron gate. Finally. We were home.

During our first week in Kenya, we drove this same road (in the opposite direction) when we delivered the ambulance to Tenwek Hospital. We thought it was great fun to flash the lights and sound the siren to scoot dogs off of the road. But that was not even close to the giggle we had as part of the presidential motorcade.

Just hours before we squirmed as we drove in first gear over ruts and in second gear over sand. What began as high stress ended with laughter of delight.

Laughter is good for the soul!

Chapter 17

Lived Among Us

*Show me your friend and I will
show you your character.*

~ African Proverb

I first met David at the close of the sixth day of our first week in Kenya. As with the sixth day of creation—"And there was evening and there was morning" (Gen. 1:31)—knowing David was good. We stayed up that first night talking until after one o'clock. He told me stories about the two years he lived with and ministered to the Pokot people. Life had been difficult. He had been bitten twice by scorpions and contracted malaria both times. A snakebite could be fatal. An infection after stepping on a thorn could get serious fast. David always faced the danger of getting caught in the cross-fire when cattle rustlers snuck into the area.

David looked me in the eye and listened intently, trying to catch every word. His laugh came quickly as our conversation progressed. As I got to know him better during our return trips, I saw that he possessed the gift of evangelism. He loved the Pokot people and worked diligently to communicate the gospel in their language and cultural context. His greatest testimony, however, simply came through how he lived among the Pokot people.

David encountered resistance by church leaders to his growing awareness that God called him to pioneer missionary work. I identified with that experience since I had faced similar obstacles. One church leader told David, "You can work among those people for five years and not have one convert." David recognized the possibility of failure but held tightly to one thing. "I will be faithful," I heard him say numerous times. "If I succeed, praise the Lord. If I fail, praise be to God. God is not calling me to be successful, He's calling me to be faithful." Faithful. I identified with that intention, too.

On his first Sunday with the Pokot people, David preached with translation from Kiswahili to Pokot and seven people responded to the invitation to follow Jesus as Savior and Lord at that first service. Karen and I met each of these seven believers.

The Pokot men did not easily receive David. In the early days they came up to David, spears and bows and arrows in hand, and just stared at him. He did not yet speak Pokot, so he just stood in silence as the men known for aggression and violence approached him in an intimidating way. He told me that he often felt afraid.

Soon after David moved to Ng'rong, the fifteen-year-old son of a Christian woman died. This woman wanted to break from the Pokot way of dealing with the dead. The Pokot traditionally have put dead bodies under a tree and even joked by saying, "There is one hyena for every person." The Christian woman wanted to express respect for her deceased son, so she asked David to help her bury her child. He did. The only tool they had was a hoe. These two worked all day in the hot sun, but were able to dig down only three feet. They wanted to go deeper, but physical and emotional exhaustion sabotaged further effort. At the end of the day they buried her son in the shallow grave and piled rocks on top.

David immediately suffered the consequences for helping this woman. He had violated the Pokot tradition. For the next month, not one Pokot man spoke to David. If David came near, the Pokot men walked away in silent protest. David had moved to Ng'rong to share the gospel, but it is difficult to do so when people avoid you.

Once when David used the local "taxi" (the tractor and trailer), the drunken driver went over a rough patch that caused the trailer to flip. David tried to jump to safety, but when he fell to the ground the trailer landed on top of him. The fact that he fell into a ditch probably saved his life. He could not move or crawl to safety without the trailer being lifted. The others on the trailer robbed David and left him to die. Fortunately he did not have any broken bones and eventually made his way home.

Several weeks after moving to Ng'rong, David suddenly started speaking Pokot. As I have reflected on this, I believe that God gave David a spiritual gift. The effectiveness of his ministry increased as David began to speak to the Pokot in their language.

David eventually began three preaching points in addition to the congregation in Ng'rong. He walked to the various locations to encourage the Christians there. I installed a prefab building in one of the remote places.

David persisted in the face of obstacle after obstacle. On one occasion he escorted three teenagers to a youth camp. They walked eighteen miles to catch the transport truck that would take them to the camp. The truck never came. So David and these three teens walked forty miles to the camp.

One Sunday afternoon, Karen and I accompanied David as he visited people from his congregation. We stopped at the home of a young woman who cared for her grandmother. The woman told me, "Several years ago I heard the Jesus man." This statement intrigued me. I wondered if she heard Jesus in a vision. "But David is different," she continued. "The other people left in their helicopter. David stayed with us." Ah, she heard the "Jesus man" in a film. A mission team swooped in, set up the equipment, showed a film in the Pokot language, counted converts, packed up the equipment, and flew away.

But David lived among the Pokot. He felt the fear, and held steady. He faced the intimidation and rejection, and remained available for God's mission. A veteran missionary sustained him with a visit once a month, providing food and companionship for a few hours. David told me the first time I met him how lonely he often felt, but he remained faithful.

David embodied the gospel. David listened first, loved sincerely; he did not lead with spoken words. His persistence prompted him to go shirtless among the partially clothed men, to wear flip-flops made of old tires. He did not hide the fact that he came from a different tribe, but he sought to live as a faithful follower of Jesus transplanted in a new culture. David gave witness to "the Word [who] became flesh and lived among us" (John 1:14) through a gracious, compassionate presence long before his words made much sense to some of the Pokot people. David may have exhibited the Incarnation more fully than any other person I have met.

Our first project in Ng'rong involved building a house for David and his soon-to-be bride. We constructed a four-room house using stone for the walls and metal for the roof. There were two bedrooms, a living room, and an inside kitchen. We included an inside shower room. There was no running water, of course, but we installed a drain in the floor that carried greywater to the base of a nearby tree. A person could shower with a bucket and cup.

We returned to Ng'rong seventeen days after the long journey to Tenwek Hospital when Karen broke her leg. Gladys, David's bride-to-be, traveled with us on this return trip to

Ng'rong. This was her introduction to Ng'rong and the Pokot people. James Ouma, one of the workers on our construction team, traveled with us too.

Exuberant joy greeted our arrival in Ng'rong. We could not have anticipated such an enthusiastic welcome. When the women saw Karen had returned to Ng'rong, they started whooping and clapping and dancing. When we left on the morning less than three weeks before, the somber mood cast a shadow over everyone. No shadows on our return; only dazzling sunshine. I may never experience such joy again this side of heaven.

We soon discovered that the Pokot women assumed they would never see Karen again. They knew the seriousness of Karen's injury. Several had been nearby when it happened. They knew firsthand how fragile life could be after such an accident. Karen's return may have been a resurrection from their perspective.

I saw evidence of another resurrection. There stood the fourteen-year-old girl who suffered with complications during the delivery of her baby. When I left her at the rural hospital, the outcome looked bleak. But she made it!

Gladys's introduction to the people with whom she would soon live could not have been more spectacular. Our main objective for this trip was to finish the house. We came to install kitchen cabinets, paint the inside walls, and hang interior doors. But something much more important occurred in the moments just after our arrival. Gladys saw up close and personal the good people who for more than two years her husband-to-be had humbly served in Jesus's name.

I wondered how Gladys would manage living in such a remote place. As a child, her parents provided a comfortable home. By joining David in Ng'rong, she would be living in a world vastly different from what she had known. I should have saved my energy. After David and Gladys had been married about one year, they spoke at the church we attended in Kericho. Perhaps eight hundred people heard them describe their ministry with the Pokot people. I remember Gladys's testimony that day; "I feel more at home in the Kerio Valley than I do in Kericho." She learned the language and seemed totally comfortable with the Pokot women. I suspect that the good start she had when she stepped out of the 4×4 on her first trip to Ng'rong helped set the course. Karen's relationship with the women opened the door for Gladys.

David and Gladys held their wedding ceremony at the village school. We drove the bride's attend-ants that day. More than a year prior, we slipped into the sealand container a four-by-twelve-by-twenty-inch box filled with artificial flowers from our daughter Sher'ri's wedding. We had no idea when we packed the container how they might be used. The day had arrived and a little bit of Oregon added beauty to the Kenyan wedding.

I was surprised as I watched a school classroom turned into a slaughterhouse. They killed the cow and skinned it right there. They left the hide lying on the floor and used it as a work area. I watched as piece by piece they removed the head, intestines, and feet. As pieces were trimmed off of the carcass, they used a tree stump and a sharp machete to chop the meat into stew-size pieces, bones and all, just like the butchers did in Dessalines, Haiti.

For the meal, groups were assigned a room in the school building. A sign above one classroom, for example, indicated that David's relatives would eat there. Men from the family guarded the door so an uninvited guest could not crash the wedding party.

The best part of the day, however, happened just before the wedding began. I was surprised—and so happy—when a truck pulled onto the school grounds with about thirty Pokot people standing in the back. Somehow David's Pokot friends scraped together the money to hire a truck and driver. They probably walked from Ng'rong to the trading center, and then stood in the back of the truck for hours to attend the wedding of their pastor. What a great moment!

During the reception, just before they cut the wedding cake, guests were invited to speak words of blessing. An older Pokot man spoke. He called David his son. He pledged to keep David and Gladys safe and secure.

I immediately recognized the miracle. Kipsigis and Pokot people are not supposed to like each other. Kipsigis children are threatened that the feared Pokots will kidnap them if they misbehave. But here this Pokot man spoke with love for David, a Kipsigis.

I wondered if the church leaders who opposed David going to Ng'rong remembered their own words as they listened to the old Pokot man. I hope so. I hope they repented because of their lack of faith and courage.

I may never see a more perfect example of Jesus bringing together people known for animosity against the other. David, a pioneer missionary, took the risk. He loved the people. Like the believers in Ephesus, in Kenya, too, "now in Christ Jesus you who once were far off have been brought near by the blood of Christ. . . . So then you are no longer strangers and aliens, but you are citizens with the saints and also members of the household of God" (Eph. 2:13, 19). That is true. I saw it with my own eyes at a wedding in Kenya.

David is my hero.

The wedding celebration ended just as the heavy afternoon rains arrived. I remember rolling up the pant legs of my suit, getting out of the vehicle, and twisting the dial on the front wheels to engage the four-wheel drive. I was drenched by the time I got back into the car, but I needed the extra traction to get out of the mud pit.

About the same time, the truck with thirty Pokot friends pulled out of the school grounds. They, too, were soaked. I paid special attention to a young mother who carried her infant child standing in the back of the truck. For hours she would stand holding her baby as that old truck rattled down the road. After the long journey to the trading center, she and the others would set out for Ng'rong, walking mile after mile. These people truly loved their pastor ... in response to the love he demonstrated when he came to live with them.

Chapter 18

Tea Time

If you want to go fast, go alone. If
you want to go far, go together.

~ African Proverb

Karen has the gift of hospitality. I have known that for years. Mostly because of Karen, we welcomed people into our home long before we moved to Kenya.

When our girls were in grade school, Karen made Sunday the best day of the week. Sunday dinner was a big deal at our house. The girls could invite friends to join us for the afternoon and we would meet up with their parents that evening at church. We often had other guests with us, too, sometimes a spur-of-the-moment decision as we left the church building.

Years later, when the youth pastor from our church lived in our house while we were in Haiti, they had a family member visit them. When the visitor saw our family photo on the wall, she asked, "Who are those people?" When she heard that it was the owners of the house, she replied, "I know them!" It turns out that for a while she lived on the streets of Portland. Sometimes she attended our downtown church on Sundays and on one occasion came home with us for dinner.

The gift of hospitality proved to be a key element while living outside of the United States. As I gave attention to the work project in a rural Kenyan village, for example, Karen interacted with the people of the congregation. While I kept the workers busy and safe, Karen talked to the friends from the community who came to watch. While I monitored the workmanship, Karen prepared our meals. We formed a great team. Karen created a comfortable environment for persons from the United States working with us on short-term mission teams, too. These people walked into a cultural context very different from their own, and Karen's hospitality provided a bridge that helped them make the transition more easily.

Karen nurtured our relationships with the men who worked with us on the church roofs in Kenya. Out of everything we accomplished in those years, one of the things I cherish most involves how a diverse group came together as a highly effective construction crew. Karen played a key role in making that happen. I can show this best in a story.

About midway through our time in Kenya, we had enough money to buy a ten-year-old pickup truck to use with the construction projects. This small, double-cab Toyota had a winch on the front and a hitch on the back. We could squeeze five of us into the cab and still pull the tandem-axle, twelve-foot flatbed trailer.

On one particular morning we loaded enough metal roofing to cover a thirty-by-sixty-foot church building, a heavy load. We had been on the road for about an hour and a half when we came upon a stretch of road recently leveled with a road grader. Heavy rainstorms came through just days before our trip and turned the roads into a soupy mess. The dirt in that area was clay that stuck to a person's feet making the shoes get bigger and heavier with each step.

We came to a small river just before arriving at the church. The bridge crossing the river consisted of two big trees with heavy timbers for the planks, the whole bridge about sixteen feet in length. I came over the ridge going too fast for the conditions. I applied the brakes. They locked. We slid toward the river in the slippery mud. The heavy trailer started pushing our little pickup. When we came to a stop, I looked out the right window and saw my trailer beside the truck. There we sat, jackknifed, four feet from the bridge. The whole thing happened in just seconds.

We sat in silence for a moment, then I said to the group, "Well, we might as well have tea time since it looks like we'll be here a while." Karen and the three workers with us that day laughed, an anxious laugh.

Tea time was a big deal for our workers. We knew that they often came to work on an empty stomach, so in addition to Kenyan tea with lots of milk and sugar, Karen often fixed hard boiled eggs, fresh fruit, and cooked sweet potatoes. On this day, the trailer was the right height for a table, so Karen spread a tablecloth on top of the sheet metal and served the tea. We took about forty-five minutes for tea time that morning. By the time Karen repacked the ice chest and folded the tablecloth I had figured out how to straighten the tangled mess. Thirty minutes later we arrived at the building site in a good frame of mind, even with the delay, because of the gift of hospitality.

We discovered that many people in Kenya did not know their actual birth date. Instead, people tended to pull a date out of thin air. Further, birthday celebrations were not common. Karen tried to change that. For each of the men who worked with us, Karen told him to invite four or five friends for dinner. She made a birthday cake. We spent many wonderful evenings this way.

When we lived on the Bible college campus, we started having movie nights at our house. We had a VHS player and a television set. On a couple of Friday nights each month our house filled with students. A college professor asked me if students were watching movies at our house. When I told him about our Friday night parties, he said, "I thought it was you. References to movies are starting to show up as sermon illustrations in the preaching class." I am not sure how someone could work the Three Stooges into a sermon.

We eventually put a covered patio on the backside of a house we built on the college campus. Two poles came up through the tabletop to support an eight-by-fourteen-foot thatched roof. A long retaining wall created a bench that provided additional seating. The house was on the campus property line and overlooked a pasture, so we had a bit of privacy. This served as a wonderful gathering place for college students or short-term mission teams who came to work with us. Regularly I saw Karen's gift of hospitality lovingly offered to all.

Karen had a vital ministry especially with the women students. Sometimes they just made cookies. Since most of the young women did not have access to an oven, Karen bought the ingredients and invited ten or twelve women to come over to bake and decorate cookies. Each woman went home with a plate of cookies. Another time we took photographs of each woman. We helped them make nice picture frames too. The women then had a Christmas present for their parents.

Through these types of relationship-building activities, Karen became a trusted confidant to many of these women. In the Kenyan culture, the grandmother was the one to talk with girls about sexual matters. As people left the family village for a larger city, some of the young women had few opportunities to talk with their grandmothers. Sometimes the grandmothers spoke only the tribal language and the girls spoke only English or Kiswahili. Often the relationship between the grandmother and the granddaughter was so undeveloped that conversation about sensitive matters would not occur. On occasion Karen filled the role traditionally held by the grandmothers for these women students.

Karen heard stories difficult to comprehend. In one of the first Bible studies Karen had with women students, they talked about forgiveness. The women engaged in good discussion around the biblical passage. Suddenly one of the women spoke with great emotion. She told about her father calling his brother saying he was returning to the town in which they had grown up. He called his wife to say he was cleaning out his office. He never made it home. Someone killed him before he could leave the office that day. The police called it a robbery gone wrong, but the threats he had received previously seemed to indicate otherwise. "I know nothing about forgiveness," the young Bible college student said.

Another young woman came to Karen for counsel. Both of her parents had died. A married sister was her only living family member. Each time she went to her sister's house, her brother-in-law pushed her toward sexual relations. He was insistent. She felt trapped. So she talked with Karen about the situation. "When you go to your sister's house," Karen said, "I want you to go straight to your brother-in-law and tell him that you have told me about what he is doing. If he doesn't change, tell him that Madam Swanee will find him."

The girl was stunned. Finally she said, "Do you love me that much?" Karen's willingness to defend her friend answered the question even before the young woman verbalized it.

We encountered a lot of abuse of girls and women in Africa. Too often the patriarchal culture seemed to condone the mistreatment of women. In one event that received international media attention, 306 boys attacked girls in a school dorm. Nineteen girls died; seventy-one were beaten and raped. The headmaster of the boys school told newspaper reporters that the boys did not intend to kill the girls, they just wanted to rape them. Evidently in the mind of this school official, rape is acceptable as long as it is not accompanied with the intent to do lethal harm. Newspapers repeated the story on the fifth anniversary of this atrocity. I anonymously posted the article near the student mailboxes hoping to generate conversations.

Many times when we prepared to leave a country, our friends told us that their security was leaving too. Who would defend them if they had conflict with a neighbor or were accused of stealing a cow? Who would advocate for them if a family member got sick and needed medical care? We did not set out to do so, but discovered that just our presence provided an umbrella of security for people at the bottom of the social or economic or political ladder. Maybe they never had to rely on our influence in five years, but they knew we would stand with them and speak on their behalf.

The brother-in-law stopped harassing the young woman.

We had just returned to Kericho after Karen's first trip to Ng'rong following the accident. Both of us were dead tired. Four of the eight days on the trip, Karen suffered with a small stone stuck in the walking cast. She slept in the tent, like always, and cooked our meals. She helped paint the inside of the house. The cast slowed her down a bit, but it did not bring her to a complete stop. The foot swelled during the trip, so she may have done too much too soon.

When we got home, Karen cleaned the camping gear and went on a search-and-destroy mission for the ticks in our luggage. I worked in our makeshift office, sketching a design for a food storage building we would construct in a few months and balancing the checkbook. At 10:15 p.m. I turned off the adding machine and the light. *Enough for this week*, I thought to myself.

I climbed into bed and snuggled with my wife, as much as you can with a person wearing a seventeen-pound plaster boot. I closed my eyes.

"We really need to be praying that God will give us the right words to say to [a couple we knew]."

I responded immediately. "I'm tired of carrying other people's burdens," I said. "Why should I take on their problems?"

"Because their problems are your problems, too," Karen replied. "If people have needs and you don't see or know about them, then you have no responsibility. But if you have eyes to really see, God knows you have seen and their trials are now your trials, too."

Silence followed. Karen soon fell asleep.

As I laid in the darkness, wide awake, I remembered the night we slept in a church basement in Seattle after I read Proverbs 24—"Don't try to disclaim responsibility by saying you didn't know about it. For God . . . knows you knew!" (Prov. 24:11–12 TLB). I started thinking about people, not building projects and bank balances.

Karen planned a big party as my fifty-fourth birthday approached. About forty guests joined us in the dining room at one of the two hotels in Kericho. This was a diverse group. Two Hindu brothers and their wives were there. They owned the hardware store where I purchased building supplies. They also owned the plant where Kenyans brought their milk for processing and packaging. The Sikh man who owned the machine shop came to the party with his wife. The Muslim restaurant owner and his wife attended. Professors from the Bible college, African church leaders, and Bible school students were present. Of course the men who worked on my construction crew were there. I am not sure of another occasion when such a varied collection of people assembled in Kericho.

Karen planned for an open mic time. She envisioned people talking about how they met me and describing my quirky mannerisms. We were surprised when one of my workers,

Elkanah, jumped up to speak first. Elkanah and I enjoyed a good relationship. He called me Dad. I took that as an honor since his parents had died. Now he stood to address the whole group.

"The best thing about Dad is Mom."

Everyone started laughing.

This response shocked Elkanah. "No, I'm serious," he said, "the best thing about Dad is Mom. She baked a cake for me. That's right, she made me a birthday cake. Nobody loves me like Mom."

Elkanah unknowingly set the tone for the whole evening. Karen thought people would enjoy having a little fun at my expense. Instead, person after person talked about the joy of being together. No one used the word, but they really described hospitality. The group at this birthday party that in many ways had so very little in common, laughed together as good friends do. Hindus, Sikhs, Muslims, Christians—a wonderful gathering of people loved by God.

The next morning I stopped by the hardware store. Both Indian brothers stood behind the counter. One of them immediately said, "The best thing about you, Swanee, is Karen." They began to laugh and told the story to other men working in the store. For weeks afterward, I often heard someone who had been at the party remind me that the best thing about me was my wife.

Elkanah got it right.

Chapter 19

Mom and Dad

Sticks in a bundle are unbreakable.

~ African Proverb

My primary task in Kenya involved assisting rural congregations with the construction of church buildings. No one else with World Gospel Mission in Kenya had the time or expertise to do what Karen and I could do. We quickly developed the strategy where the local congregation built the walls up to the ring beam and I brought in a crew to put on the roof. I always preferred to work *with* a congregation rather than merely doing something *for* them. Thanks to the generosity of friends in the United States, we finished dozens of church buildings at no expense to the local congregation.

Once the congregation completed the walls, I went to the work site to measure the building, designed the roof structure, and began to compile a materials list. On one project, Karen held the end of a one-hundred-foot measuring tape so we could check the width at one end of the building: twenty-nine feet. Karen stayed put and I walked to the other end to get a measure of the length: sixty feet. Karen joined me at the far end to check the width: a little over thirty feet. *Okay, what is going on here?* We double-checked our measurements and confirmed that the building was one foot wider at one end than the other. We made the roof trusses thirty feet long and had a six-inch overhang on both sides of the short end. After that experience, when possible, I helped the congregation lay out the building before they dug the footers to make sure we ended up with a square building.

The people of a congregation joyfully received us when we arrived at a job site. They took good care of us. On one trip, a woman confided that I was the first white person to stay in her house. Her excitement made it difficult for her sleep at night. She asked me to stay another night because she thought she could finally relax enough to get some sleep. I told her that if we stayed longer she would kill all of her chickens trying to feed us. The old mamas in the church were a delight.

On one of the very few times that I traveled without Karen, I had four workers with me in a very rural area. If everything went well, I calculated, we could finish the roof in three days. That meant only two nights away from home. My workers were delighted to discover that the pastor had jury-rigged a small television set powered by a series of car batteries. The first night we stayed up late watching a 1998 World Cup soccer match on a grainy black-and-white TV.

The house had two rooms, a living room and a bedroom. My workers slept on the floor of the living room. I shared the full-size bed that nearly filled the bedroom with the pastor. I awoke at one o'clock in the morning to the sound of the pastor snoring. A strange rattle accompanied each inhale and the bed vibrated with each exhale. I was trapped between this roaring machine and the wall. I wiggled in hopes that he would roll over. No luck; he kept up the snarl and bellow. I complained to myself that once again I ended up in an uncomfortable situation.

As I lay on my stomach, I reached next to the wall and began to pull at the seam of the mattress. I finally succeeded in tearing a hole in the very corner. Then digging inside the mattress cover with my fingers, I ripped off a piece of foam rubber that became two earplugs. Sleep came quickly after that intervention. The next morning I dropped the improvised earplugs into my pocket since I expected to need them for night two. I got away with the crime. Probably by now a rat has been convicted and sentenced to death for the destruction of property.

To make tea the Kipsigis women dropped dry tea leaves in boiling whole milk. They would make tea in a five-gallon milk can and expect us to drink it all. Between the caffeine and the sugar, we had plenty of energy after a few cups of tea.

We never could predict what might happen while working on a church in a rural village. On one occasion, I climbed the scaffolding to get on the roof to begin the workday. A few minutes later I heard someone rattling the scaffolding. I looked down to see a man of about my age and size. I watched as he went to the gas generator and pulled out the electric cords.

"Who is this guy?" I asked a local person.

"If you don't give him money," they told me, "he will break things."

I quickly did an assessment. While in college I volunteered at the state school for persons with mental disabilities. This man seemed to be in his right mind. He was just a bully.

While church members fished out coins from their pockets to pay off the extortionist, I climbed off of the roof and slipped up behind him. I grabbed the man in a bear hug. I thought I would have the advantage because of the surprise factor, but he put up quite a struggle. After a couple of minutes I was able to maneuver him to the front gate. When I pushed him onto the road, he turned to face me. I did not say anything. I shook my head and pointed down the road. To my great relief he quickly turned and walked away. The church people were laughing as I returned to work.

The next morning laughter broke out again. Someone told me to look at the road. There he stood. He had come back, but he did not come through the gate. I again shook my head and pointed down the road. He squinted his eyes with a disgusted look on his face before he turned to continue down the road. Again the church people started laughing. I told them that I needed to act foolish to deal with foolish people. I was certainly glad he walked away because I did not want another wrestling match with that man.

I often took a new soccer ball with me on trips. If possible, I would give a nearby school the soccer ball. At a school assembly, I would hand the soccer ball to the school principal and encourage the students to be diligent in their studies. I took a new soccer ball with me on one project but discovered that the school had already closed for the Christmas holiday. The road near the church consisted of two narrow paths for the tires to follow. After one workday, as I drove slowly on this road, I noticed a ten-year-old boy playing soccer with a ball of rags. This kid was good; he could keep the rag ball in the air with just his feet. I stopped the truck in front of his house. My worker who spoke Kipsigis called the boy over and presented him with a brand new soccer ball. The look on his face was pure joy. We wished him a merry Christmas and drove away.

The men in the back seat called for me to stop because they saw a man take the soccer ball away from the boy. I backed the trailer down the road as quickly as possible and found the man of about twenty years still holding the ball. The young boy stood crying. I told the man to return the ball to the boy. I said that I would come down the road again the next morning and if the boy did not have the ball I would find him to set things right. The boy came to the job site the next day, still smiling and holding his soccer ball.

The week after we installed the last piece of sheet metal roofing on this church building, the congregation asked if we would return for a celebration. We took three missionaries with us that Sunday. One missionary asked how the congregation could get grass to grow inside the building. That explanation had two parts. First, in this part of Kenya it rains three hundred days a year. Second, the walls of the building had been up for many months waiting for the roof. The combination of those two things resulted in a wonderful, green carpet on the floor of this rural church building.

As is sometimes the case in the United States, raising building funds comes easier at the beginning of a capital campaign. Many congregations in Kenya could raise enough money to get the walls up, but struggled to finish the project. That is where GAP International played a key role. What seemed like an impossible task for a local congregation became achievable through the partnership with friends in the United States. I was glad to be able to facilitate that collaboration for scores of church buildings in Kenya.

I generally hired local workers to help me on the building projects in Kenya. Even when we went to the remote areas like Ng'rong, most of the time Africans traveled with me. I could accomplish much more when I had a good team than I could working alone, and I could help them by providing income and training.

I always liked it when my work team consisted of people from various tribes. I found tribalism so strong in Kenya, even within the church, that I consciously tried to break down some of the barriers between people.

On one project I took with me five men from five tribes: Kikuru, Kipsigis, Kisii, Luhya, and Luo. Members of the congregation welcomed us warmly when we arrived, but seemed a bit surprised at the diversity of our team. A Kenyan can quickly identify a person's tribe by the last name, so with the introductions our diversity was uncovered.

The woman who arranged our sleeping arrangements pulled me aside. "Sir," she started, "I am so sorry, but there has been a misunderstanding. We have only one house for all of you to sleep in."

"That's okay," I said.

She did not believe me, so she said it again. "We have one house. I did not expect to receive people from other tribes."

"Thank you for what you have done for us," I replied. "We get along well and one house is just fine for all of us." I still am not sure she understood. She probably watched us carefully that week.

Unfortunately, I heard similar things from church leaders. Some persons did not approve of the diversity on my work teams. They wanted me to favor men from their tribe. When Christian missionaries first came to Kenya, one denomination started churches in one area and another denomination started churches in another area. For years Christians could stay within their tribal structure. They rarely confronted their prejudice against Christians from other tribes.

I decided to push against discrimination whenever I could in whatever form it appeared. My crew provided a natural place to start.

Elkanah Mwangi was Kikuru. Elkanah experienced a hard life. His father got in a fight with a man and broke the man's tooth. The man told Elkanah's father that it was okay and they started drinking together. When the father was drunk, the other man doused him with gasoline and lit a match. After his father's death, a local political leader offered to buy the family property from Elkanah's mother. His offer was significantly lower than the value of the property, but his mother had little recourse but to sell. She was from the wrong tribe and had no leverage with which to negotiate a fair selling price. Elkanah worked for a man from his church for eighteen months. They cut trees for firewood and Elkanah developed calluses on his shoulders from carrying logs. The man paid Elkanah just a little, but regularly promised him that the proceeds from the next truckload would be his. That never happened.

I liked Elkanah's work ethic. One day the two of us worked on the back of the trailer to offload sand. After our shovels had been flying for a while, we stopped to catch our breath. With great enthusiasm, Elkanah said, "Dad, don't you just love to sweat?" Another time I asked if he could do some painting. Elkanah laughed, put his head on my shoulder, and said, "You know I can do that." I guess I should have asked *would* he do the painting, not *if* he could.

There were moments when Elkanah did not know if he would finish Bible college. At times it was concern about having enough money to pay the tuition. Other times it was because of his academic struggles. When he graduated, he wanted me to see his transcript. "Do you see right there?" Elkanah pointed to his transcript. "This is where I met you. And all those times you wanted to see my grades; no one ever asked me that before. I did not want to disappoint you."

After Elkanah graduated from college, he became a teacher. When he received his first paycheck, he brought treats to the workshop for a celebration.

Joe Engoya was Luhya. His older brother was enrolled at the Bible college and their father served as a Quaker pastor. Joe had trained as a welder, but he told me that he did more welding on his first day with me than during the entire welding program at a technical school. Joe lived in one room near the workshop and often ate dinner with us.

James Ouma was Luo. I met James when I worked at Africa Nazarene University in 1991. He came to Kericho as a student at the Bible college and I was glad to have him on my work crew again. (I tell more of James's story in chapter 22.)

Edwin Milley was Kipsigis. Edwin may have weighed one hundred ten pounds, but he could easily carry a ninety-pound bag of cement. For many months I struggled to get Edwin to join the conversations. Over time he became a good team leader. On one occasion the team completed a project in three days under Edwin's leadership when I expected it would take a week.

Michael Saiar was Kisii. I first met Michael at a service of a new Free Methodist congregation. He wore a white patch over one eye that day, the result of a construction accident. Michael was an excellent welder. He contributed to our work by building steel windows and doors, handrails and benches.

Eric Betts was Kipsigis. Eric was a neighbor of Philip, the man who worked on the household chores with Karen. When one short-term mission team was with us, Karen needed an additional helper and Philip recommended Eric. One day with the same mission team I needed another man to keep the project on schedule and Karen reluctantly allowed Eric to go with me. I asked if he had ever been on a ladder. He had not. I asked him to climb the ladder and walk around on the roof so I could see if he might be comfortable with heights. He kicked off his shoes and went right up on the roof. We found him a leather nail apron and hammer, the other men instructed him on how to nail sheet metal roofing, and in minutes he pounded nails like a pro. Several weeks later I asked Eric to keep track of how many hours each person worked and how much they should be paid. At the end of the week he brought me a handwritten ledger with columns so neat you would have thought a computer produced it.

This team developed into a first-class construction crew. We could have made a lot of money in the United States; we did excellent work in an efficient manner. The thing I liked the most, however, revolved around how we surpassed the cultural expectation that people only associated with others of their own tribe. We proved that diverse people could work together on a common mission.

A visitor from the United States observed how well these guys worked together. Impressed with their faithfulness, joyful spirits, and teamwork, this man offered a gift of five hundred dollars per person as a way to honor these good men. I suggested we use these funds to encourage them to save money.

I called a team meeting. I explained that if they would save twenty dollars a week, a friend would also add twenty dollars to their account. So if a worker saved five hundred dollars, he would end up with one thousand dollars. In those days the Barclays Bank paid seventeen percent interest. I took out a calculator and showed them the increase seventeen percent could make.

I explained that they could have the funds from the monies they saved at any time. The matching funds would be available to them only to buy tools or other items to setup a business, to buy land, or to get married. The five hundred dollars matching funds were for their future, not to buy a television to watch the World Cup.

Phillip asked the first question that indicated he understood what I proposed. "So," he said, "you mean that I can buy my own land and I won't have to keep farming with my cousins?" He got it. Philip was also the first to make a withdrawal. Philip's neighbor needed to sell a pregnant cow. When he came to us with the proposal, he told us that if he owned a cow we could buy our milk from him. And if the cow gave birth to another female, he would soon have two cows to milk. I remember the morning Philip told us that the night before his cow had delivered a female calf. As the workers listened to Philip's story, everyone could see the value of saving money and making choices that contributed to a more secure future.

This generous gift set a new direction for our crew. When we left Kenya, Edwin, Eric, and Michael formed a cooperative to buy many of my tools. They transitioned from laborers who relied on the boss to contractors who sustained themselves. After returning to the United States, we received several color photos of the buildings these three friends had constructed. I was thrilled.

The members of our Kenyan work crew called Karen and me, Mom and Dad. From my observations, we were unique when greeted in such a familial fashion. A professional distance seemed to be the norm for other missionaries, professors at the Bible college, and the medical staff at Tenwek Hospital. But living together 24/7 changes a relationship. We traveled in the same vehicle. We stopped for tea time together. We shared lunch out of the same ice chest. We used the same outdoor toilet. Sometimes we slept in the same room.

On days when the crew and I worked in the shop on the college campus, sometimes we walked up the hill to the college dining hall for lunch. Karen and I sat with our workers eating rice and beans. Students watched us and knew that Karen and I ate the same cafeteria food that sometimes prompted their complaints.

When we traveled or shared a meal, we asked the workers questions about their parents and siblings. I learned that only one man did not come from a polygamous family. Even at the Bible college, only a few students had only one mother. These men quickly told us about how much they loved their mothers. They described what their mothers had done to keep them in school and to provide food for them to eat.

Most men sat in silence when we asked them about their fathers. Some freely admitted that they had no desire to be like their father.

At times we invited our workers to be our teachers. We might ask something like, "Did it surprise you when you heard him say that?" or, "What does this mean in your culture?"

We faced awkward situations on occasion because of our relationship with our workers. The fifty-fourth birthday party was an example. I sometimes felt uncomfortable when the workers related with me so casually when missionaries or college professors were present. For some reason it did not feel right for me to be friends with my workers when others did not have such a personal relationship. We lived in a way contrary to that of the Muslim, Hindu, and Sikh business owners, too. They never shared a meal with their employees.

But Elkanah, Joe, James, Edwin, Michael, and Eric were co-workers, not employees. When we needed help, we looked for persons to join the team.

In many ways, I realize, I acted like a father to these young men. I provided security and income. I taught them to think logically and not to allow frustration to influence their response in difficult circumstances. I never had a flesh-and-blood son of my own, but in the end I had many sons. I was proud of each one in ways that matched their personality and strengths. I felt so blessed for the privilege of watching these young men become responsible husbands and fathers who lovingly cared for their families. Even if no one in Kericho called me Dad, I still would have been honored to be a friend of such fine young men.

Chapter 20

Advocate

Do not follow a person running away.

~ Kenyan Proverb

In the middle of 1998, Karen and I were in full swing with our work of putting roofs on church buildings. During this time almost every Saturday we hired two to five Bible school students. Sometimes we worked on maintenance projects on campus. Other Saturdays we prepared building materials for a trip we would take the next week or worked on a local church project.

We employed students for various reasons. First of all, this gave us the chance to get to know the students. We also employed the students because they needed money. They could work on a Saturday and earn a little money to buy toothpaste and other personal items. I also believed that we could help students learn the benefits of doing manual work to counteract a culture that tended to cast laborers as inferior persons. We became good friends with many of the students. The students began to trust us and seek our help on occasion.

One day a couple came to me seeking assistance. Both the husband and the wife were students at the Bible college. A

184

twelve-year-old girl had come from their home village to care for their child when both parents had classes at the same time. This family lived in an apartment complex very close to the campus and with the girl available for childcare both of them could complete their studies.

When the couple came to see me, they said that two days before the young babysitter had gone to a neighbor's house to help with light housekeeping. When she returned they immediately noticed that she did not seem like herself. She had stopped talking. The couple started asking questions and eventually drew out the story. While she worked at the neighbor's house, the middle-aged man raped the twelve-year-old girl. When our friends took the girl to the police, the law enforcement officers did not believe the girl's story, dismissed them, and took no action. The couple came to me for assistance.

I believed the girl, even if the police did not. I knew of a young girl raped in Haiti who stopped talking, psychologically unable to cope with the trauma, so when I heard that this girl did the same thing I was convinced she spoke the truth. I told the couple that I would help as I could. Many times I did not like the clout given me as an American in Kenya, but on this day I would seek to use any power I might have for the sake of a girl who had no standing in society.

I picked up my friends at their apartment and, with the young girl, we drove to the police station. Some twelve-year-old girls look and act like a fifteen-year-old; others like a nine-year-old. This girl seemed younger. We rode quietly as I drove to the police station.

When we walked into the building I immediately felt hopeful that we would get action because a woman officer sat behind the counter. When asked to talk about her experience, the girl looked at the ground. She spoke with a quiet voice. Her English skill suggested that she had not completed much schooling. When the girl came to the end of the story, she said that the man gave her two dollars "in appreciation" and for her promise to keep it a secret.

I could tell from the look on the officer's face that as she heard the story she felt compassion for the young girl. This officer assured us that the man would be arrested, which we later heard occurred that same day. I think the female officer was the key to justice in this case. I took the young girl to the hospital for a physical examination where she had to go through the whole story again, quietly spoken as she relived the trauma one more time. She had physical injuries no girl should ever endure.

On a Saturday about two weeks later, a woman walked into the workshop. She dressed very nicely, carried herself like a professional woman, and spoke like she was educated. She introduced herself as the sister of the man in jail for the rape of the girl. In a most sincere manner, she asked me to go to the police to arrange for her brother's release so he could go back to work. She said he was an administrator for the department of education.

I told this woman in a very direct way that I wanted her brother to remain in jail. I went on to say that when he gets out of jail he needed to go work on a farm and not around children.

She begged for mercy. Since just the two of us stood in the workshop at the moment, she spoke with an urgency that might not have been there with others present. She said that she and her brother were orphans and that they had experienced great difficulties in life. She went on to say that her brother tried to be good, but sometimes it was impossible.

I listened to her plea, and then gave her a suggestion. I said that perhaps her brother should be castrated if he could not control himself.

That shocked her. Of course she thought of my suggestion as a bizarre idea and told me that it would accomplish nothing.

So I told her a story. I once owned a dog that would not stay home, but that he never strayed after he was castrated. I suggested that if it worked for the dog maybe it would help her brother, too.

She turned and left in a huff. I watched her go, then went back to my work.

Three weeks went by and I heard nothing about the rapist. On a Saturday morning, I worked with about twenty people to prepare to pour a concrete floor for a school building next to a church. While I worked on my hands and knees, preparing concrete forms, a man walked toward me. I stood up as he introduced himself as the man who had just been released from jail.

My anxiety went up. He was big. He stood too close. I was not surprised that he found me; any street kid could tell you where to find the man who pulled a trailer. The rapist easily located me on this Saturday morning.

"Just because you are a rich man," he said, "you think that you can come to Africa and throw your weight around."

I sized up the man. He was at least six inches taller than me. I said, "Just because you're a big man, you think that you can rape a twelve-year-old girl."

The contrast between the man and the girl could not have been more vivid. He spoke as an educated man; she spoke with halting English. He dressed well and carried himself with a degree of sophistication; she stared at the ground when she spoke. He stood at least eighteen inches taller than she did and exuded power and authority; she was fragile like a small reed on the sandy riverbank.

The man was correct in that I would gladly use my "weight" to protect a little girl.

The conversation took an unexpected turn and started down a new road. The man told me that while he sat in jail thieves broke into his house and stole his propane tank, gas stove, television, and mattress. Then he accused me of being the thief.

I laughed. "Why would I work six days a week to help others, then at night break into people's houses? Why would I steal your stove? I have a gas stove and I don't need another one. I'm not a thief. You must be crazy to accuse me."

As we talked the man slowly moved closer to me.

"My sister told me that you think I should be castrated like a dog."

Oh, my. I heard a threat in the man's statement, so I reached into my pocket and took out my red Swiss army knife. I opened the big blade and began to strum the blade with my thumb. I looked eye to eye with the rapist.

Then I became aware of a person stepping up next to me. Edwin was one of my workers, a young married man with a small child. He was almost touching my elbow. Then Eric stepped alongside of me. Eric was twenty-five years old, strong and wiry. Michael stood next to Eric. Michael was married with three small children. His hands were rough like a tree branch.

No one said anything. There we stood, four men positioned shoulder to shoulder, staring down a rapist. The stand-off lasted just a few seconds, but the intensity of the moment made it seem longer. The rapist blinked first. As he turned and walked away, he called over his shoulder, "I'll be back."

"We will welcome your visit," I replied. I put my knife back in my pocket.

We all laughed as we watched the man walk away, an anxious laugh, not the kind that refreshes the soul. I never heard what happened to the criminal case against this school administrator. Two times I went to the school offices and plainly told the officials that this man should not be working near children. I do not know that my efforts met with any success.

Could I have used my knife to cut the man? I do not know the answer to that question. Did the rapist think I would actually harm him? I do not know that either. But the knife probably had less to do with the coward's retreat than the fact that my friends stood beside me. They, too, opposed the abuse of a young girl.

Very soon after moving to Uganda I recognized the dire conditions of the people in this country. After a visit in 1908, Winston Churchill dubbed Uganda "the pearl of Africa." When I arrived in 2003 the people still staggered with the consequences of the ruthless rule of Idi Amin. Most of the men on my work crew had seen extensive suffering. One came from a village where ninety-seven percent of the adults died from AIDS. The government built a fence around this village to keep residents in and visitors out. Another worker and his sister were the two survivors of a family of twelve. He grieved as he told me that his sister grew increasingly weak. These men had only seen death; their experiences left little room for any notion of life. Abundant life was beyond belief for these men.

The seeming lack of aspiration to improve living conditions bewildered me. The desire for knowledge seemed to be nonexistent at times. After working with about seventy-five men, I could only identify two who really engaged in becoming better workers, better men. All the others only did what they had to for a little money to buy sunglasses or shoes or a mattress. We visited a rural church one Sunday where only five children out of two hundred attended school. My experience in Kenya was vastly different from the situation I found in Uganda.

After I complained about hearing the thumping bass from the loudspeakers at a nearby club until almost sunrise, I learned that the night life in Uganda had a link to the Amin regime. In those difficult days, when a man needed a haircut or to fix a flat tire, he could do so more safely at night than during the day. If a mother needed to buy vegetables, she went to the street vendor at night. The habit had been set, so even after the end of the conflict, extensive activity at night continued.

Drinking and promiscuity increased with the night life in Uganda. Before starting work each morning, I led the twenty-five workers in a devotional. At least once a week I brought an article from the newspaper on AIDS. HIV-AIDS articles appeared in the newspaper every day because it touched every person in every part of the country. An old African man told me that he believed the spread of AIDS had a direct link with alcohol consumption. "The more people drink," he said, "the more sexual activity. The more sexual activity, the more AIDS deaths."

When I talked with my crew about AIDS, some of the men blamed the West for the epidemic because the Western nations did not spend enough time or money educating people of the danger. When I heard this line of reasoning, I went around the group and asked every man if he knew how AIDS was transmitted. Of course they knew. I said that what Uganda needed was a spiritual awakening that would change the hearts of the people. Education can help, but they needed a movement of God to transform them.

I found a fatalism in Uganda that I had not seen before. "Life just happens," people said. "There is not much I can do to change the circumstances. If my time to die is February ninth, then I will die." These people had little sense that they could make decisions today that would alter tomorrow. That fatalism fed a lawlessness where anyone felt justified to do whatever without concern for how it affected others.

Soon after moving into our first rental house in Uganda, our worker, Wilson, and I heard a commotion down the street. We went to investigate and found an angry crowd threatening a man who had retreated to the attic of a house under construction.

"He raped a fourteen-year-old girl," someone told us.

"We went to the police station," another added, "but they refused to come."

Wilson and I hurried back to our house, got in the car, and drove the half mile to the police station. The police listened to our call for assistance, but suggested that we pay them to leave the office. Wilson finally convinced the police to do something. When we returned to the mob scene with the police officers, the rapist was trying to hang himself in the attic while the crowd below shouted and threatened him. The police eventually subdued the man and hauled him to jail. I do not know the fate of this man. I suspect he paid a bribe to the police and was released.

Wilson and I found the girl and her mother. The mother had brought food to the work site to sell to the men constructing the house. The rapist asked for a second dinner. When the teenage girl delivered the food—unfortunately no one else worked in the house at the time—the man assaulted her. People in the crowd told us that the man had been with a prostitute the night before, so we immediately worried about the girl being infected with HIV-AIDS.

Wilson went with me as I drove the girl and her mother into Kampala to seek medical help. The convoluted system required us to go from office to office, paying a fee at each place. The next day we took the girl to the hospital for the care she needed, then back to the doctor with the hospital report. Only then did we get the prescription for the medicines the girl required. I hope in a small way she felt empowered and worthy, like a human being created by a loving God, and not like an object to be exploited for momentary sexual pleasure.

I am appalled that authorities like the police turn away from women and children when they most need assistance.

What grieves me even more is that I have known church leaders to do the same thing. These Christians who should know better seem to ignore God's call to "Rescue those who are unjustly sentenced to death." We cannot just "stand back and let them die" (Prov. 24:11 TLB). I know how uncomfortable it is to seek justice. I have images in my mind of a young girl in a quiet, halting voice describing the details of a rape. Her anguish continues to haunt me. Sometimes I wish I could just forget the whole thing, but once it is in the brain it stays there. When we find a troubled person, we need to share the pain, even if the anguish troubles our spirits.

Early one evening just before dark, the girl's mother stopped by our house to thank me.

One day in Kenya, I pulled to the side of the road to allow a farm tractor and trailer to pass. We shared a narrow road with room for only one vehicle at a time. As I waited, I noticed four women sitting on stools about twenty feet from me. They sold food items. A primary school was nearby and the children bought bananas and candy as they walked to and from school.

Just as I started moving again, as I began a left turn, I noticed the woman on the far right of the group had a man yelling at her. I could not see his face; his back was toward me. I could not understand what he said, but it was quite evident that he was angry.

Quick as a flash, this man kicked the woman in the head above her left ear. He kicked her head like it was a soccer ball. She fell off of her stool and lay in a fetal position.

I jerked the emergency brake on my pickup, jumped out, and ran toward the man. Just before he kicked the old woman again, I caught him around the chest with my right arm. Then I lifted him over my right hip and threw him to the ground. My strength in that moment surprised me.

The man hit the ground hard. He landed on the ground with such force that his body bounced. I saw his head ricochet off of the hard dirt.

As he lay on the ground, motionless, I got my first look at his face. He appeared to be about twenty-five years old. He seemed to be several inches taller than me, medium build. But it was his eyes that I remember. His eyes were wide open, but not moving.

Did I kill him?!

The old women gathered around me. They thanked me for what I had done. They helped their friend back to her feet, the one who had been kicked in the head.

The man on the ground still did not move. I prayed earnestly as I looked into his open eyes. For long moments I could think of little else but that I may have killed a man.

I cannot clearly account for the timing, but perhaps two minutes went by before the man on the ground began to wake up.

The old woman said I was a hero. I did not want to be a hero. I just wanted to protect her.

I went back to my pickup and drove away. I promised myself to never again jump out of my truck and throw a man to the ground. In my mind I repeatedly heard the sound of his body hitting the ground. Over and over I saw the look of his open but unmoving eyes. I remembered listening intently for his breathing.

The next day as I worked on the building project, a young man came to the job site with a woman about his age. This man looked familiar to me but I did not immediately know who he was. Then he said, "People tell me that yesterday I did something very bad to my mother, but I don't remember. I had been drinking. I wanted her to give me more money and she refused."

The man I had knocked unconscious never mentioned anything to me about the incident. Instead, the three of us discussed his drinking problem and I urged him never to touch alcohol again. I told him I saw him kick his mother. He listened to me with his head down and said he was sorry, but he refused to promise never to drink again.

When the young man and his sister left, I did not have any sense that they had ill feelings towards me. I took a risk. I acted impulsively, dangerously, to protect an old woman. That time things turned out okay.

We moved to Kericho, Kenya, when I was fifty-two years old and my hair was turning gray. I soon discovered that both my hair color and my age were assets. Almost always when walking into a new social situation, within the first three or four sentences I came to expect a personal question: in what year were you born? The man asking the question was searching for an "age mate." If I was born within five years of his birth, either younger or older, the celebration of finding an age mate began. I have even had a man go to the door and announce to the women cooking outside in the makeshift kitchen that their guest was his age mate. If more people arrived later to join us for the meal, I would be introduced as the host's age mate. Later in the day, men gathered in small groups according to age and the older men invited me to join them because I was an age mate. Being an elderly man in Kenya really was a big deal.

I developed very strong opinions about a few issues in Kenyan culture: female genital mutilation, the high dowry that young men must pay before they marry, and the exclusion of young men in most social situations. When I became aware that the older men had the last word about these matters, I enjoyed sitting with them and looking for polite ways to venture into these controversial topics. It often started with a question asked of me about American culture, but I tried to turn the discussion back to Kenyan culture.

One day I stood in the courtyard area of a cluster of homes when I started hearing loud screaming. I looked to where the sound came from, about fifty feet from where I stood. I had never before heard such a desperate sound and I asked what was happening. They called it "female circumcision." The term "female genital mutilation" better describes the practice. I can think of few things so awful. On this day they cut a girl who had just completed the final term of school. In this horrendous practice, women force a girl to sit in cold water, an ineffective anesthesia. Then they hold the girl to the ground while one of the women uses a razor to remove some or all of the girl's genitalia. A terrible tradition.

I talked about this one day with an age mate; I will call him William.

"We must circumcise the girls," William told me, "because without this they would be worth nothing."

Girls are worth nothing without being cut?

"No man wants a wife who can have pleasure with sex," William continued. "She would be no better than a dog going here and there looking for sex."

Because William served as a church leader, I felt free to bring God into the discussion. "God created both male and female," I said, "and the Bible tells us that God said his creation was good. I have been to many countries, and this is the only place where I have witnessed this awful practice."

"But no man will want to marry my daughter if she isn't circumcised," William said. "To get a good dowry, she must be circumcised. She would be worthless without it."

The money necessary to pay a dowry can sometimes total several years' wages. A young man going to Bible college will not be able to provide the dowry expected by many fathers. I had come to believe that the dowry system put undue hardship on young men. "Why do you need so much money for a daughter?" I asked.

"I want to convey to the man that my daughter is very valuable," William said. "I want the man to know my daughter must be treated with respect."

I nodded in agreement. Then I presented William with a scenario. "What if ten years from now your son-in-law has proved to be a wonderful Christian man. He has provided well for your daughter. She is safe in a nice house. He is a good father. The family is active in the church and you see your grandchildren growing up to love the Lord." I paused, and then looked William in the eye and asked, "Now will you give the money back to your son-in-law that he paid in the dowry?"

William's face took on a bewildered look. What I suggested did not even seem to be within the realm of possibility in his way of thinking. "Of course not," William insisted. "The money has to stay with us. If we give the money back then he could immediately start treating our daughter harshly."

After a good laugh, I told my age mate that I believed he loved money too much. It seemed obvious to me that he loved money more than he loved his daughter. Condoning female genital mutilation to get a good price for your daughter? I did not buy that logic.

Our challenging conversations never seemed to have an adverse effect my relationship with Kenyan age mates. They seemed to enjoy my company. I had the skills and tools to install roofs in remote locations, something quite expensive for the church leaders to do on their own. They wanted to do business with me, so they listened to what I said, even if my words planted seeds of doubt about their cultural practices that, at least to me, seemed contrary to the Christian scriptures. They kept coming back for further conversations.

College students and young church leaders agreed with me on many of these matters. But what could they do? Old men dominated the culture. These old men had years of experience but very little understanding of their children.

With my age mates I sometimes pointed out that in Genesis 12 we learn that Abraham left his family home in obedience to God and in Genesis 2 God said that a man and a woman were to leave families to cleave to each other. "God wants you to become one with your wife," I said, "not one with the other men in your tribe. I understand that you need to have a strong clan, but the extended family can be strong only as individual family units are strong. You need to care better for your wife and teach your son to care for his wife, too."

I kept trying to chip away at the brick wall that surrounded the good ol' boys club. I wanted them see how they pushed the women to the margins and how they even excluded the younger men from their conversations about important issues.

"If you go to the store the next Saturday to negotiate with the Indian to buy metal for a new roof," I said, "his son will listen to the conversation. We all know that it is not proper for this young boy to interrupt his father during a business negotiation, but the boy is listening. Am I right?"

No answer.

"You know I'm right," I continued. "As a father you put your son at a huge disadvantage when you do not allow him to hear your conversations. You go off with your age mates and leave the young people out. In very practical ways, the young men in Kenya suffer because their fathers have not trained them. When a man negotiates to buy a motorcycle, for example, the Indian businessman will have the advantage every time because of how the Indian has been trained by his father."

I sometimes wonder if I did any good with these matters and think I should have done more. I hope my example provided a hint for the men I worked with that they could live in a way that honored others, especially women and children. I hope I encouraged a young couple not to back down when injustice must be confronted. I hope a young girl began to hold her head high with dignity because my effort to protect her demonstrated her worth. I hope the college students who worked with me on Saturday mornings learned how important it is to get involved with social issues, especially for the weak whose voices are often ignored. I hope my friends know deep in their beings the power that comes from standing shoulder to shoulder against those who would harm and maim.

Chapter 21

Rejoice in Hope

A friend is someone who knows the song
in your heart and can sing it back to you
when you have forgotten the words.

~ Kenyan Proverb

The call came while Karen and I worked in Caracas, Venezuela—"Simeon died suddenly in the hospital." Simeon and I had forged a great friendship during the eleven months I worked on the construction of Africa Nazarene University. I had listened to Simeon preach; he persuasively presented the gospel. Just before we boarded the airplane for the trip home, Simeon handed me an envelope. After I got settled in my seat, I opened it to find two neatly typed pages. I read, in part, "I will always remember our work and laughter together."

I remembered, too. After I received the news I had to find a quiet place in Caracas to grieve the loss of my friend in Nairobi. Pneumonia, they told me. I wondered about his widow, Pamela, and the four children.

When we moved back to Kenya a couple of years after Simeon's death, as soon as we could we made contact with

Pamela. Every three or four months Karen and I drove from Kericho to Nairobi and met Pamela and the children on a Sunday morning at the Central Church of the Nazarene. We sat together during the service, afterward sharing the noon meal together at a fast-food restaurant. The four children always looked good, nicely dressed and wearing clean shoes.

One Sunday we had sufficient time after the meal to take the family to their house. After our visit, as we drove away from the house, Karen and I were close to tears at what we saw. The house sat in the middle of a slum and was not a safe place for children. Pamela's younger sister lived with them, so six people shared a room no more than twelve feet square. Furniture filled the space: a double-sized bunk bed, one mattress on supports above the main bed; a beat up, red sofa; and a coffee table. They sat on the bed and sofa to use the coffee table for meals. We had no idea our friends lived in such a dangerous location with so little.

When we heard that Tenwek Hospital had a job opening for a cafeteria manager and cook, we rushed to Nairobi to drive Pamela the six hours to apply for the job. She met with a committee that utilized an interesting interview process. They left Pamela in the kitchen with flour, salt, potatoes, bread, cooking oil, and other food items with the instruction that she prepare lunch for them.

Pamela smiled broadly as she walked toward us after the interview. "This job is mine!" she said. "They will never find a better cook than me." We knew her confidence was well-founded. She got the job. Pamela made a quick trip to Nairobi to pick up a few personal items, arrange for the care of her children until she could make living arrangements near the hospital, and immediately returned to Tenwek Hospital to begin her new job. The world looked so much brighter for Pamela. We rejoiced with her.

About five days after Pamela started at Tenwek Hospital, one of the hospital administrators remembered that Pamela had not completed the health assessment. So Pamela went to the lab to provide a blood sample.

That same day, personnel in the hospital lab started telling people not to eat in the cafeteria. "The new cook has AIDS," they whispered. When Pamela heard what people said about her, she packed her bags and found public transportation back to Nairobi. Later that day a hospital administrator called us to apologize for the conduct of the lab technician. Pamela deserved to learn of the lab results in a more appropriate manner.

Very early the next morning, Karen and I left Kericho for Nairobi. We found Pamela very angry. "Because I am a Luo," she said, "the Kipsigis at the hospital do not want me to work there. That is why they spread this rumor about me."

We listened to her rage. When it seemed appropriate, we suggested that she have another blood test in Nairobi. She responded with great enthusiasm to the suggestion.

We arrived at the Seventh-day Adventist Hospital a few minutes before noon, just as the offices were closing for lunch. We put a bit of pressure on one of the American staff members who finally agreed to draw blood and start the lab work. We went back for the results after the lunch break.

The hospital worker handed Pamela a small piece of paper, about the size of a three-by-five index card. As she held it in her hand, we could see the words "HIV positive" written on the card with an ink pen. The person writing the lab results traced over the word "positive" an additional time to darken the dreadful message.

We stood there in shock. After we started for the parking lot, when we stepped outside the front doors of the hospital, Pamela's legs could no longer hold her up. Karen and I helped get her to the car. When we closed the car doors, we finally had a bit of privacy in which to try to begin to process the news. My mind moved so fast that I did not know if I could even drive the car, so we just sat in the hospital parking lot for a long time.

I remembered a conversation with a person who wondered if Simeon died of AIDS. Pneumonia was the presenting issue, but AIDS could have been a factor.

I kept running through various scenarios as I tried to imagine the road ahead. Each thing I thought of involved suffering.

Pamela expressed her anger with God. "I have been faithful to God since I was a young teenager," she cried. "I have been faithful, but God was not."

Karen and I resolved to give attention to Pamela's spiritual life. We might have little we could do to save her physically, but we resolved not to lose her spiritually.

Pamela wondered about her children. Their father had died. Now she found out that she had AIDS. How could she care for her four children when she was sick? What happens to them when she dies?

As we sat in the car, weeping, suddenly I visualized the heavy load of responsibility added to our shoulders. Karen had been correct on that night months earlier; Pamela's pain became my pain.

Karen and I left Nairobi after Pamela promised to keep in touch by phone. She could use the telephone at a funeral home where her cousin worked. Within a few weeks her health became a factor in the children's well-being. Sometimes the children stayed home from school to care for their mother.

We gave Pamela money to try to ease the burden. We finally realized that Pamela and the children did not need money as much as they needed us. It is true: there are some things that money cannot buy. That was when we decided to move the family from Nairobi to Kericho where we could be nearby.

On Thursday, August 6, 1998, Karen and I drove from Kericho to Nairobi. Our primary task involv-ed moving Pamela and her four children to Kericho where we could assist with her care while she was ill. Since we were in Nairobi, we planned to shop for food and auto parts, visit the dentist, and Karen needed a haircut. James Ouma rode with us to Nairobi. We dropped him off at a busy intersection. He would find another way back to Kericho since our car would be filled with Pamela and her family.

Our friends, Vic and Darlene, stayed at the guest house, too, so on Friday Darlene went with Karen to a hair salon at a shopping center and Vic ran errands with me. We were glad for this time to be with our friends especially since they would return to the United States soon afterwards.

Vic and I drove through downtown Nairobi earlier in the morning. On our way back, we encountered heavier traffic as we made our way through the center of the city. We still moved forward, but it was slower. I had just driven through the traffic circle near the United States Embassy on my right. I heard a dull boom, not a sharp sound like a firecracker or rifle shot. My 4×4 rocked violently in sync with the boom, from right to left. This was a heavy vehicle. I regularly used the 4×4 vehicle to pull the trailer loaded with heavy building materials. Whatever just happened had a jolt to it. I checked the rearview mirrors. I thought maybe someone in an out-of-control car rammed us from behind. The concussion took my breath away. I felt like the air had been sucked out of the open windows of the 4×4.

In my confusion, I opened the door. As I stepped out, I watched sheets of glass from the twenty-five-story Cooperative Bank building float down like someone stood on a balcony and tossed a deck of cards into the air. Unsuspecting persons on the sidewalk below could not run fast enough to escape the falling debris. Dust filled the air.

I jumped back in the 4×4 and told Vic it must be a fuel truck explosion. Vic said, "That's bigger than a tanker truck. I think that was a bomb."

I wanted to leave the area quickly, but that became impossible as chaos engulfed us. Cars and buses rushed from the scene. One bus had the side blown in. A small car jumped the curb and tore off the oil pan. Drivers tried to make u-turns, further scrambling the traffic. I watched a pickup truck try to get away, the back full of bloodied people. Vehicles hit each other like bumper cars at an amusement park.

All around me I saw people running, screaming, bleeding, falling down. Some ran toward the embassy. Some ran the other direction. People running right and left. To my left, several children ran by. The smallest, maybe about six years old, fell into a hole about two feet deep that utility workers had left uncovered. I watched with a sinking feeling in my stomach as the child cried hysterically while the other children ran away. I felt so powerless to help in the chaos. The child climbed out of the hole and ran off . . . alone . . . in the same direction that the other children had gone.

Vic and I stayed in the car. When a bit of space opened, I pulled the 4×4 forward. Inch by inch, we moved away from the bomb site, but chaos continued to surround us. We saw people running even after we made it a mile away from the disaster. People reported that they heard the blast ten miles from the city center. I later learned that we were about seventy-five yards from ground zero, on the other side of the embassy building from where the bomb detonated. If traffic had been heavy enough to cause me to be a few seconds slower, I would have been even closer to the detonation.

For the next hour, Vic and I slowly made our way toward the shopping center where we had left our wives. We commented on how everything seemed to be moving in double time, but how long it actually took to make progress. We could usually make this trip in a few minutes. No groups stood on the street corner in casual conversation that day. When we finally got to the shopping center we watched CNN and saw that we had survived a truck bomb and heard reports of the initial emergency response. We did not alter our plans for the weekend, but we did have to take the long way to get where we needed to go.

Later we learned that terrorists threw a stun grenade at a guard in the parking lot at the United States Embassy, hoping to get the explosive-laden truck through the gate into the compound. People in nearby buildings rushed to the windows to investigate the sound of the grenade. When the bomb detonated moments later, the blast implanted shattered glass into faces and eyes of those standing at the windows. About 4,650 people were injured; 213 died.

We had no way to know about James Ouma since this occurred before we had cell phones. We heard his story three days later, after he returned to Kericho. Ironically, he probably could have seen our 4×4 since he was at about the same place on the same street. James was near the train station, just to the left of where we sat in traffic, when the blast went off. The explosion blew clay tiles off of the roof of the railroad terminal.

James immediately tried to help the injured around him. Among those he assisted was a man lying on his back, eyes closed, face covered with blood. When James knelt beside the man, the man opened his eyes. "Are you James Ouma?" the man asked after getting a good look at his rescuer. James had stopped to help his uncle.

As you might imagine, people throughout Kenya talked about the bombing. People wanted an eyewitness report so when asked I briefly described the suffering I witnessed. Many people told their friends who told their friends. My father contacted a columnist for *The Oregonian*, the major newspaper in Portland, who ran a story on me.

I did not welcome the attention. My own survival did not dominate my thoughts in those days. My friend, Pamela, had the awful disease that would soon leave her four children as orphans. I continued to hear the echoes of screams from frightened people. I saw images of bloodied people frantically running. I could only imagine the psychological scars inflicted on a six-year-old child trying to get out of a two-foot hole in the midst of a stampede. My own situation seemed so insignificant compared with the trauma I saw all around me.

The Sunday after the bombing, we drove Pamela and her four children to Kericho. We rented a two-room house for them not far from the Bible college campus. We helped Pamela provide a relatively normal life for her family. Karen and Pamela had many good days in the kitchen. I loved the smell of their cooking. Even more, I loved the sound of the laughter that filled our home. We included Pamela and her children in our lives and enjoyed the opportunity to introduce them to our friends in Kericho. We had more than a year of good times together.

Two of the Kipsigis church leaders questioned why we brought a Luo family to Kericho. They clearly worried that this added responsibility would take me away from the busy schedule of installing roofs on rural church buildings. I chafed at what seemed to be un-Christlike assumptions and misguided priorities. But they formed a minority on this issue. Other Christians in Kericho joined with us to care for Pamela and her kids. In the end, the church functioned as God intended during those days.

We eventually began thinking about long-term care for the children. Karen and I recognized that we could not become the parents to four African children, so we looked for other options. Over time, this family of five made a big impression on the people in Kericho. Two families in particular took an interest in the children and talked with us privately about adoption, but we could not work out the details. It saddens me that tribal differences too often became a factor.

When Pamela began to need regular medical care, we found a Luo doctor who worked at one of the tea estates. He took a personal interest in Pamela and saw her several times even though doing so was an exception to his work agreement with the tea company. We appreciated this man's kindness.

Pamela began to have a distended stomach. Then the doctor told us that her liver had failed. Finally he said that he could do no more from his office, and that she should go to a hospital in Kericho. The doctor spoke with great compassion and profound clarity. Pamela's life would soon be over. No one shed a tear in the room when the doctor gave us the prognosis. We drove the ten miles back to Kericho in silence.

Karen and I were busy with a work team from the United States while Pamela lay in a hospital room. Some of the women from this team went with Karen to visit and pray with Pamela. Death seemed very near. To our great surprise, one day Pamela sat up and started talking. She asked Karen to bring her some beef soup. Pamela told Karen, "I'm so hungry I could eat a whole cow by myself!" Later that day, Karen and the women from the team took the soup to Pamela and she ate a lot.

All four of her children visited with their mother. Pamela talked with each one privately. She urged them to be faithful to God, to be obedient in school, and to listen to Momma Karen and Papa Swanee. I think the thirteen-year-old son may have been the only child who realized his mother was near death. The other children just knew that their mother was very sick. The children showed very little emotion even when they kissed their mother before leaving the room.

We prayed for these four children. We asked God to help them feel protected and secure. They were just kids!

Pamela died soon after she blessed her children.

The work team joined us at the funeral service. Afterwards, Pamela's family placed the casket in the back of an open pickup truck for the two-hour trip to her home area near Lake Victoria. The four children stayed in Kericho with friends of the family. Karen and I continued hosting the work team. Our minds often drifted away from our regular responsibilities and toward the interment occurring many miles to the west.

Karen and I felt like our own child had died and left us with four grandchildren. In the early days following Pamela's death, most of the time we were too busy to think about our grief. Even one hour to sit and collect our thoughts was something we could not seem to find. Grieving our great loss seemed only to come in bits and pieces. Something said in church as we sat with the four children, for example, might cause tears to flow. I never knew what would trigger my grief.

About one week after Pamela's death, the oldest son came to our house. Karen asked if he was doing okay. "I'm fine," he replied.

Karen thought a moment, then said, "I miss her terribly. When I'm in the kitchen . . ." Karen did not finish the sentence. The boy began to cry.

The youngest daughter always wanted to sit by me on the sofa while we watched a video. She found ways to sit next to me at church, too. I learned to expect that eventually this young girl would lightly touch my hand. I would look into her beautiful, dark eyes and form a slight smile. That became our private signal that it was okay for us to hold hands. This young girl needed a father. I was the lucky guy!

We explored various options to find care for this family. Nothing seemed promising. A few families assisted for a while, but could not continue for various reasons. We located boarding schools, but a permanent solution did not materialize at first.

A few months after Pamela's death it became clear to me that Karen could no longer continue to function the way we had been. The poor road conditions we often traveled only increased her back pain. The turning point for me came on the second day of a wildlife safari with a work team. Karen told me that she decided just to rest at the camp and not go to see the animals. I knew how much she enjoyed a safari, so I interpreted her decision to stay at the camp as an indication that the pain had reached critical levels. Beginning that day I looked towards returning to the United States.

Once we both knew it was time to leave our good life in Kericho, we took up the ultimate responsibility of finding a stable place for the four children. We had not asked for this task, but we never wished the load just to disappear. These children did not create a problem that we needed to solve. Instead they were our great joy to know and love.

We knew about the Testimony Faith Homes (TFH) located in Eldoret, Kenya, because some of the orphans from TFH enrolled as students at the Bible college where we lived. We liked the fact that it was homes, plural. This Christian ministry cared for orphans in several homes with a mother and father present in each house. The organization also operated a first-class school for children in Eldoret, so the orphans had access to excellent education. TFH also made the commitment to help the orphans go on to college or technical school after graduation from high school.

We first moved the two boys to TFH. On a weekend after the boys were settled, we took the two girls to see their brothers. As we pulled onto the campus, the youngest girl announced, "This is where I'm going to live." We did not have the courage to tell her that that would not be possible. She had tested HIV positive. TFH policy disallowed anyone with HIV from living in one of the homes.

Later on that visit, as we watched the four siblings play together, the founding missionary said to me, "I feel bad that they can't be together." That started a series of conversations

209

that ended with the two girls joining their brothers at the Testimony Faith Homes. A turning point in the granting of an exception came when the missionary director said, "If she gets too sick to live in another home, she can live in our house until she passes." I am so glad this man made the personal commitment so the family could stay together.

Before we left Kenya, I took my work crew to the Testimony Faith Homes for several days. We repaired windows, trimmed trees, and completed other maintenance tasks. The men who worked with me knew the children. After this trip they saw that the children would be well cared for in the years ahead. I had traded the pickup truck for a Land Cruiser. I gave the Land Cruiser to Testimony Faith Homes when we left Kenya.

We had been on a long, painful journey. Karen and I still weep at times when we remember Simeon, Pamela, and their four children. But we also see evidence of God's faithfulness. That causes us to "rejoice in hope" (Rom. 12:12).

Chapter 22

African Sons

A friend is someone with whom
you share the path.

~ African Proverb

Karen and I met with the workers on our last day in Kericho. While we sat inside, it rained outside and the workers started telling stories.

We marveled at the fact that no one had a serious injury during any of our projects. We had plenty of opportunities for something to go wrong given the ladders we climbed and the metal roofing we handled and the welding we did, but our wounds involved just minor burns, cuts, and bruises.

We laughed at the rural pastors who were extremely uncomfortable with me doing manual labor. On more than one occasion a pastor told my co-workers to take a shovel out of my hand or to take the wheelbarrow away from me. "Do not let the white man keep doing this work with his hands," they would say. And they shook their heads at how I dressed: old shirt, shorts, and tennis shoes. If the sole of a shoe began to flop, I wrapped it with duct tape until I could get home for another pair. Clearly these pastors did not understand the privilege of manual labor the way I did. On that wet day in Kericho, we enjoyed remembering our times together.

I met James Ouma in 1991 while working at Africa Nazarene University (ANU) in Nairobi. I soon learned that James was a highly skilled welder. Because James lived on the ANU campus, we spent many evenings in conversation. I quickly discovered his love of reading. I got him books out of the library since I could check out books, but he could not. We discussed the ideas he discovered.

When we moved to Kericho in 1994, we started looking for James and found him serving as a pastor. I affirmed his gifts for ministry—we saw that clearly during our time together— then used an illustration to make a point. I told James that if he was cutting firewood maybe the first thing he should do each morning would be to sharpen the ax. As a pastor, maybe he needed to prepare well. I suggested that James visit us in Kericho, walk around the campus of Kenya Highland Bible College, talk with the professors, and consider starting college. He accepted our invitation to come see us in Kericho.

When he joined us for lunch after his campus tour, he announced, "I want to come to this school." He went on to describe how he wept when he saw the library. "When I saw all of those books," he said, "I realized how little I know. I want to learn." Karen and I joyfully paid James's school fees.

During the second week of his first year, James told me that he was having a difficult time processing all of the new ideas that came flying at him in class lectures. He said that he rushed back to his room after a class, covered his head with a blanket, and repeated everything said by the professor. He did not want to forget anything, so he verbalized the concepts to get a better grasp of the subject. James also told me that as a child, his father had forbidden him to speak in the house, or to even be in the house when other men were in conversation.

James said that he could see the words in his mind, but sometimes he had difficulty verbalizing what he thought. James worked diligently to overcome these challenges.

Since James could not produce his high school records, the Bible college would not enroll him in a degree program. He eventually completed all of the course work for a degree, but only received a certificate because he could not provide documentation of his previous education.

As a boy, James walked seventeen miles one way to attend primary school. For high school, he went to Kampala, Uganda. In those days, the army loyal to Idi Amin terrorized the country. One time James asked me if I had seen people being murdered or women violently ravished. I told him that I had not. Then I asked if he had witnessed such things. He described the violence he saw as a teenager. One time, soldiers robbed him of his backpack and watch. James told me that as a high school student he spent one weekend at a hospital complex hiding from the soldiers. He left the hospital early one morning for the shores of Lake Victoria where he could catch a boat to his family's house in a remote village. Because of the political unrest during his high school studies, he did not have a transcript necessary for him to be a degree-seeking student at the Bible college.

A Bible college professor came to Karen and me one day. She said, "I am not sure what you two will accomplish here in Africa. Only God knows that. But maybe the best thing that you have done to serve God's kingdom is to bring James Ouma to school. That man is a sponge. He pulls information from me." James finished Bible college at the top of his class.

James went from Bible college to Naivasha, Kenya, to plant a church. One evening James attended a revival service held at another church. Afterwards, James met a young woman who needed someone to walk with her to her home since it was unsafe for an unaccompanied woman to be out at night.

James volunteered. James asked her what type of books she liked to read. Her answer impressed him very much. A friendship formed between James and Carolyn.

As the prospect of marriage increased, James asked Karen and me to accompany him to negotiate the dowry with Carolyn's family. When we mentioned this invitation to our missionary friends and the Kenyan church leaders, every one advised us to stay away. People told us that the potential in-laws should not know of James's connections with us, that the dowry could be increased if they suspected we might subsidize what James could provide. We heard horror stories about knock-down, drag-out family feuds during the negotiations.

Karen and I listened to our advisors, but we ultimately did what they told us not to do. If we failed to accompany James, he would go alone. No one from his family would do it, not an uncle or a brother. We could not stand back and watch James go to meet the family alone. James had extremely difficult experiences as a child and a strained relationship with his father as an adult, so we served as his family in the negotiation.

None of the three of us knew what to expect. On the day of the dowry meeting, we put on our best clothes and drove in our recently washed car. We arrived at a single-story, three-bedroom house made of concrete blocks. Several cars were parked in the yard. We arrived exactly on time, but the festivities were well underway when we arrived. We felt like we attended a family reunion. At least thirty people filled the house. Karen stood with the women in the kitchen until the meal was served. James and I mixed with the men clustered in groups of four or five.

We enjoyed a wonderful meal. I anticipated that the conversation about the dowry would begin after they cleared the tables, but the topic of money never came up. We never felt interrogated or put on the spot. No one demanded that we answer personal questions or make guarantees.

Carolyn's grandfather sat in the corner during the whole time Karen and I were there. We learned later that the grandfather made it clear to the family that James was his selection for Carolyn's husband. In the conversation that happened after we left, the parents and uncles agreed that James needed to provide a modest dowry.

The grandfather died before the wedding. For a wedding present, the family gave the newlyweds living room and bedroom furniture equal in value to what James had given the family as the dowry. Carolyn's family treated James very well. I rejoiced.

The wedding was held in Carolyn's home church and her family made up more than half of the guests. A large group from the congregation James served as pastor attended.

No one from James's family came to the wedding. As final preparations were made, a time of chaotic activity, I noticed James gazing out windows and doors, looking for his relatives, I speculated. James sent money to his father to buy a new suit and fare for the bus. I sat in the church on that wedding day, on a pew with ribbons tied on the ends, watching James as he anticipated his bride starting down the aisle, and wishing that he would see his father walk in, too. He never came.

I grieved for my friend.

James and Carolyn were moving to Nairobi to begin a new ministry assignment. After the wedding reception, we loaded their furniture and belongings on our trailer. We finished saying goodbyes after dark and left for the city. It was past ten o'clock by the time we arrived in Nairobi, tired and hungry. A gasoline station was still open at that hour, and they sold us soda and pizza warmed in a microwave. On that busy road in Nairobi, with Carolyn still in her wedding dress, we sat on a concrete bench eating limp pizza in the dark.

Our wedding gift to the newlyweds was four nights at a guest house in Nairobi. Karen and I stayed there too. We moved the furniture into the house they had rented, but most of the week we lived like tourists. We went to the Nairobi National Park to watch the big animals. We did some window-shopping and ate lunch at a downtown hotel. We had a wonderful time. We rejoiced in the formation of this new family.

James regularly confirmed his ability to grasp the implications of new information quickly. He told me of his conversion to Christianity as a teenager. When he started reading the Bible, he realized that the preacher taught things contrary to God's word, so James began attending a different church. He had a keen intellect even as a young man and could efficiently sort through new information.

At one of the birthday parties Karen organized for the Kericho workers, the conversation gravitated toward the wealth of people in the United States. The group seemed surprised when I told them that poor people lived in the United States, too. I pulled out a credit card. I explained to them that the magnetic strip on the back of the card stored information about the user. This strip sent information over the telephone line to the bank if you wanted to borrow money. If the bank was willing to loan you money, then you could buy food or buy a table or put fuel in your car. "You could even buy a new Sunday suit and necktie," I added.

At that point, James asked, "What if you don't pay the bank for the loan?"

I explained the various ways a bank will deal with a person who does not make payments on the account.

James still held the credit card in his hand. "Then this card can put you in bondage," he said.

What wisdom! James, a freshman in college, quickly saw the ramifications of what I described.

James continued, "So, pastors in the United States warn people about the bondage of credit cards, don't they?"

216

Sadly, I told the group that even some Christians live in bondage because of their spending habits. James recognized the risks long before some of my friends in the United States.

James applied to a master's degree program. At first he was denied acceptance because he did not have a bachelor's degree. Then the graduate school announced that it would waive some of the entrance requirements for persons older than a certain age, with a minimum number of years of pastoral experience, and who had good grades in undergraduate study. James satisfied all of the requirements for the exemption and started graduate school as a probationary student.

James set a goal to complete a three-year program in two years. Each semester he read ahead so he could get the books from the library before all of the other students scrambled for them at the last minute.

At graduation, Karen and I sat with Carolyn about halfway back in the auditorium. Next to Carolyn sat the wife of one of James's classmates. They had taken many classes together. The wife gasped when the academic administrator introduced James as the student with the highest grade point average in the graduating class. I heard the classmate's wife say out loud, "I didn't know that James was an academic."

I smiled. My humble friend, James. Disciplined in his studies. Top of his class. For him, however, it was a simple act of being a good steward of the gifts given him by God.

After James moved to Kampala, Uganda, to serve as pastor of a church, he began to teach at a Bible college to supplement his income. The students voted him the outstanding teacher of the year. The other professors asked James to speak to the faculty on his teaching methods. James laughed when he told me about the request. He had never completed a course on educational theory or methodology. "I will need to do some research," James said, "because I need to sound very intellectual when I stand before these people." We both laughed.

When we first met James at ANU, he already provided spiritual leadership for the workers. Every morning he led devotions for the twenty-five men on the construction crew. When he was in graduate school, he awoke early each morning so he could lead the campus workers in Bible study and prayer. Kitchen staff, security guards, and landscape workers joined James on those mornings. He loved introducing big ideas about God to small groups of people.

At the party after James received his master's degree, a diverse group gathered to celebrate. Persons from the early morning Bible study came to honor their mentor. A professor attended and assured James that if James wanted to go on to doctoral studies, the professor would fully support that effort. In Kenya, a professor and the man who trims the trees do not usually go to the same party, unless they are friends with James Ouma.

After our return from Kericho and a time of rest in Oregon, we received another invitation. Karen and I accepted a call to return to Kenya for five months to prepare for the construction of a library at the Nairobi Evangelical Graduate School of Theology. The invitation came through a pastor from Illinois who had worked with us on a short-term mission team. Since the job did not require driving on rural roads, we felt like we could accept this assignment without causing Karen to experience further back pain. When that five-month assignment went well, after returning to the United States we began searching for another service opportunity with similar conditions. We ended up in Uganda.

When we arrived in Uganda in 2003, even before we moved into our rented house, a missionary asked if we were looking for someone to help out at the house. The missionary told us about a destitute pastor, Wilson, who needed employment. His family struggled financially and if he could find a steady job it would help immensely. But then a word of caution: the man had a rough personality.

Wilson's maternal grandmother raised him. One day when his grandmother sent him to get water, he encountered fighters who asked Wilson to join their effort. He set down the jerrycans, climbed into the back of a truck, and became a boy soldier at thirteen years of age.

As we worked together, I started hearing the stories. When Wilson's gun hung from his shoulder, the end hit his ankle when he walked. In the five years as a boy soldier, he never ate a meal while sitting at a table. They always ate while walking. Boys always went first when going through a forest, a human shield for the men. I heard numerous stories about the atrocities of war, actions too awful for anyone to experience, let alone a boy.

After the fighting ceased, the officers gave Wilson some money, and he accompanied other survivors to Kampala. They lived on the streets. Wilson used a black trash bag in which to sleep. Alcohol and drug use were rampant.

An old woman visited Wilson and the group of boy soldiers every Saturday. The young men mocked her when she told them about Jesus. One Saturday she said to Wilson, "Next week when I come, I want you to go home with me to be my son." Wilson never understood why she said that to him and not the others.

Surprisingly, Wilson went with the woman when she came the next Saturday. After smelling like something dead (Wilson's description of himself), he learned personal hygiene. He learned to have a meal at a table. He kicked the alcohol and drug habits. He learned to live as a disciple of Jesus. A transformation started.

Wilson eventually married. Using money Wilson received from the military, he and his wife purchased a small house. They had a Christian home and a young daughter. After years of rejection, years of hardship, life finally looked promising for Wilson and his family.

On the day Wilson made the final payment on the dowry, his wife died of poisoning. She had two brothers and, according to the Ugandan tradition, only sons shared the inheritance. When Wilson's father-in-law left one-third of his estate to his daughter, her brothers became angry. After they received the last of the dowry, they hired a person to poison their sister.

Wilson always wept when he talked about his first wife. Wilson told me that he was angry with his brothers-in-law for only one day; he then shifted the focus of his wrath to Satan and evil. He vowed to himself to bring as many people as possible to Jesus and thwart the work of the Evil One. By the time I met Wilson, he had remarried and was serving as the pastor of the Africa Gospel Church in Katale, Uganda.

Wilson maybe reached five feet six inches tall, but he would stand nose to nose with anyone. For several weeks in a row, a drunken man came into the church service in the middle of the sermon. He walked part way up the center aisle and mocked whatever Wilson said. After this happened repeatedly, Wilson instructed the ushers to keep the man outside, but the man generally got past them. On one Sunday, Wilson ran off of the platform, lifted the man on his shoulder, ran out the door, and dumped him in the road. The man's face hit the ground, and he began to bleed.

A few days later Wilson asked me if he had done the right thing. Wilson thought his actions were appropriate, but he wanted my approval. Jesus threw the money-changers out of the temple, but I do not envision Jesus rushing them, carrying them out of the temple on his shoulder, and plunking them down on the street.

We saw a rough side of Wilson in our house, too. Soon after we met Wilson, he purchased a small bag of sugar as a treat for his children. When Wilson found our watchman holding his bag of sugar, Wilson jumped him. The sugar spilled. Karen heard the noise and ran outside to find the two men wrestling on the concrete, Wilson on top and fully in control.

We now had our own experiences through which we understood the missionary's warning to us about Wilson's rough personality; his erratic behavior created turmoil for everyone. So Karen decided that she needed to tell Wilson that he would no longer work in our house. Before I left for work that morning, she told me that she would talk with Wilson that day and tell him of her decision. Karen was alone when I returned to the house that evening. We sat in the backyard as she recounted the events of the day.

As Karen prayed before Wilson arrived, Karen remembered the multiple times God had been patient with her. Karen felt impressed to offer Wilson another chance. When they talked that day, Karen told Wilson of her plan. Wilson listened carefully. He told Karen how much he needed her counsel. He told her, "I will do everything you tell me to do." Wilson and Karen made a new start.

In those days, sometimes Wilson showed up in the morning looking exhausted, so Karen told him to take a nap. That evening before he left, Karen instructed him to go directly home, not to stop to talk with people. And when he got home, Karen told him to let other family members do the talking. He needed to rest, Karen said. She told him that she did not want him coming to the house completely exhausted.

Wilson told us the next morning about the quiet evening he spent with his family. He honored his pledge to do whatever Karen told him to do. Things started to change. And Wilson acknowledged that his children told him, "Daddy, you talk too much." His marriage and family life began to improve as he began to listen.

Wilson had very little formal education as a child. He could speak several languages, but possessed only limited ability to read and write. Karen became his tutor during his pastoral training. Every three weeks Wilson spent one day in class with other pastors. He brought the materials to Karen. Many times I came into the house and found Wilson sitting cross-legged on the floor next to the sofa where Karen rested. Karen read from the lesson and Wilson repeated after her until he memorized the material. The next Sunday, Wilson used in his sermon what he had just learned.

Wilson's congregation began to grow and I designed a larger building for them. They needed to better accommodate the people coming to services each week. The old building sat in the middle of the property, so we started construction of the new building around the old. After we completed the thirty-by-seventy-foot building, the congregation quickly grew to one hundred fifty in worship on a typical Sunday.

Church leaders began to ask Wilson to preach in other churches in Kampala. In Wilson's absence from his local congregation, another man delivered the sermon one Sunday. This man announced that God had anointed him to begin a new congregation. The guest preacher urged the people to join his church. He pointed out that he had an education. Wilson did not. He reminded the people that he drove a car. Wilson rode an old, black bicycle in such bad shape that no one would even think about stealing it.

Seventy-five people attended Wilson's congregation the next Sunday morning. Seventy-five went to the school one-half mile away with the guest preacher. The guest preacher's action split the congregation down the middle.

When Wilson talked to his congregation that Sunday morning, he spoke from his heart. The guest preacher was correct, Wilson told his people. "He has more education than I do. He lives in a big house. He drives a nice car. All this is true." Wilson looked at his people before he continued. "If you want me to be your pastor, I promise you this one thing: I will never preach anything that I am not doing myself. I make that commitment to you."

But even with these conciliatory words, all was not well with Wilson.

Wilson came to our house fiery mad. The guest preacher took the sound system from Wilson's church. Wilson purchased the equipment with his own money: mixer-amplifier, speakers, microphones, and a twelve-volt car battery used as the power source. Wilson told me that he intended to retrieve it.

I began trying to convince Wilson to let it go, just to forget it, to forgive the guest preacher. I reminded Wilson that on the day of Pentecost thousands believed in Jesus as Messiah, but Peter did not need a twelve-volt battery when he delivered his sermon. The Holy Spirit energized Peter's words. Pray for the power of the Holy Spirit, I urged Wilson.

Once again, Wilson trusted our counsel rather than his impulses. He later confessed he had a knife under his shirt as he anticipated confronting the thief.

Within two months, the new church plant withered and died. Wilson's congregation continued to grow until their regular attendance reached two hundred.

One day while Wilson and I worked together at our house, we began to talk about how in the Ugandan culture a "real" man would never work in the kitchen. In that way Wilson was very different than other men in Uganda. He joyfully stood beside Karen in the kitchen to prepare a meal or to clean dishes afterwards. That was his job as a boy soldier. As we continued this conversation, an idea emerged.

Wilson privately talked with the men of the congregation. He suggested that they surprise the women and children with a big meal. Quietly the men set out to prepare the dinner to be held after a Sunday morning service. One man brought in firewood. Another provided the carrots and another the potatoes. Karen and I supplied the chicken and we helped Wilson prepare it at our house. This event required complete secrecy.

We did not attend on the Sunday of the big surprise, but we laughed as Wilson told us about it the next morning. The women and children were utterly amazed that the men served them a meal.

A few weeks later, again on a Monday morning, we had another good laugh. Holy joy is wonderful. The women in the congregation so enjoyed the fellowship at the dinner the men prepared, that they returned the favor. As soon as Wilson dismissed the congregation, women pulled out firewood they had hidden near the church and built a fire. Pots of food started arriving. The men and children quickly figured out what the women had done and danced with joy.

Wilson planted other congregations and trained leaders from the Katale congregation to serve as pastors. He told me that by the time he is an old man he wants to have planted ten congregations. I think he will do it.

Wilson and Grace had an increasing awareness of the approximately four hundred orphans living in the village of Katale. Vehicles injured some these children as they ran through the streets. Some were victimized. Very few enrolled in school, so Grace and Wilson started inviting street kids into their house during the day. They fed the children. They taught the orphans self-discipline and how to conduct themselves in a structured environment like a school. What eventually became known as the God is Good School began with ten children. As the number increased, they moved the school to the church building that I designed and constructed. After more than one hundred students attended the school, Wilson purchased land adjacent to the church building and classrooms went up. GAP International assisted with this project.

Wilson saw a need, worked in collaboration with others who could assist, and began serving the at-risk children in Katale. Wilson grew up without the nurture of a family. An old woman rescued him from the streets of Kampala. He received the benefit of persistent, stable friends who refused to give up on him. Now he blessed others in the way he had been blessed. He made a way for children to attend school, something not available to him as a boy soldier.

Wilson became effective in numerous ways and in various contexts. He led a growing congregation. He sat on a board in the community that adjudicated civil disagreements. He flourished as a husband and father. Parents came to him with concerns about their children. He nurtured kids deserted through the death of their parents or abandonment. He rallied people to provide compassionate care for those who desperately needed help.

Wilson and Grace took the lead in caring for a woman dying of AIDS who lived across the road from their house. She sometimes screamed all night. When the neighbors tried to restrain her, she fought back with a vengeance. They started calling her "Double" since she was twice as strong as any other woman they knew. At the end, as the virus took her strength, Wilson and Grace fed her. Grace stayed with her in the hospital. They shared the gospel with this woman and she died peacefully in the hope of the resurrection.

About a year after her death, while talking with Wilson one day, I connected the dots. "Double" was the one who killed his first wife. Wilson's brothers-in-law hired this woman to slip poison into their sister's drink. Wilson knew this, but that did not change anything. A neighbor needed care; Wilson and Grace provided it. In spite of the woman's past as a prostitute and an assassin, Wilson compassionately cared for the dying woman and pledged to look after the woman's teenage son following her death.

I cherish the privilege of walking with numerous young men in various countries. I have many wonderful memories of our times together. With Wilson, the transformation I witnessed could not have been more dramatic. Charles Wesley, in the hymn "O for a Thousand Tongues to Sing," reminds us that because of Jesus vivid transformations occur: the deaf hear, the dumb speak, the blind see, the lame leap for joy. John Newton's hymn, "Amazing Grace," proclaims that the lost are found. The Apostle Paul assures us that "if anyone is in Christ, there is a new creation: everything old has passed away; see, everything has become new!" (2 Cor. 5:17). I testify to the truth of these claims. I have seen a transformation so profound that it cannot be explained in any other way but the grace of God.

Both Wilson and James grew up with violence. Both men witnessed murders. Both endured the emptiness of neglect. But the stories do not end there. Christians loved them and showed them a different way to live. Through the church, the people of God, they found the family they did not have as children. And they now give themselves to extending God's love and grace to others who are like they once were.

Scores of orphans running the streets of Katale have been saved . . . literally. Through 2014, of the orphans who studied at the school started by Wilson and Grace, one hundred forty out of one hundred forty passed the Ugandan entrance exam for secondary school. These students have been equipped to join society as citizens who make a difference.

James already has contributed to the pastoral training of scores of Africans and that will multiply when he completes the doctoral studies he began in 2014. Young pastors naturally come to him for counsel. The church in Africa will be stronger because of the sharp mind and humble spirit of James Ouma.

As much as I have enjoyed retelling the stories in this memoir, I really delight in imagining the future. I like gazing out of the windshield much more than looking in the rearview mirror. I have spent much of my life trying to assist those who seek to relieve suffering by constructing hospitals, schools, and churches, but in the end I am less interested in how long a building stands than the ongoing influence of persons with whom I shared the journey.

Chapter 23

My People

One who sees something good must narrate it.
~ Ugandan Proverb

Visualize Karen and me on a remote hillside near the equator in Kenya. When we stopped the car for a lunch break, we placed food from the ice chest on paper plates. But it is more than just the two of us. We shared this meal with our friends. If you heard their last names you would know that they came from different tribes: Kikuru, Kipsigis, Luo. We so enjoyed those times with these men who became more than workers, more than acquaintances, more than friends. We were family.

Many times we heard missionaries express great delight as they anticipated family members and friends coming from "home" to visit them. We, too, enjoyed having friends from the United States come to work with us in Haiti and Africa. In 2005, a total of eighteen from the Schwanz family were in Uganda to build the Myrtle House and the Nelda House, Habitat for Humanity houses constructed in memory of my mother and sister-in-law. We have good memories of visits like that.

But something happens when you spend time with persons not like yourself. We spent years with some of our Haitian and African friends, working together, going to weddings together, having meals together, celebrating the birth of a cow together. When I started recognizing the richness of relationships, I relaxed a bit and lingered at tea time a little longer. I learned to start the day by asking my friends about their families. This was a switch for me because my natural impulse early on was to review the construction progress made the day before and describe the work goals for the day. We would get to that, of course, but only after we talked as friends. People took precedence over projects. And that is how we became family, by spending time together, by talking with each other about the important things in life, by laughing together.

I discovered that some people paid attention to skin color in places I have lived. In Haiti, children would call out "Blanc, blanc, blanc" (white) as I walked down the street. Sometimes a brave boy would rush past me, touch my arm, and yell to his friends that he had touched a white man. In Kericho, people often assumed I was British just because of my skin color. Without talking to me, they presumed I worked on a tea plantation for a British company.

I did not like being assigned to a certain slot that did not fit my understanding of myself. Sometimes I just wanted to be invisible, to move freely without being recognized as a foreigner. I wanted nothing to do with the distinctions made because of skin color. When someone singled me out in that way, I became frustrated, especially as solidarity with my friends increased. I did not like being ushered to the front of the church and being asked to preach at the last minute. I wanted to be part of the congregation, not a guest.

I suppose my mother planted the seeds for this when I was a young boy in the 1940s in Broken Bow, Nebraska. John Conrad may have been the only "colored" man in town (my parents used that term for African-Americans in those days). He owned a mule and a single plow that he used to help residents prepare the ground for their gardens in the spring. He also recycled blades from windmills to make heavy duty dust pans. I remember my mother inviting John to have lunch with us one day. John refused to come into the house, an attempt not to fuel rumors, I suspect, so my brother, Floyd, and I sat with him on the back porch having lunch together. Sometime later I saw John when my mother took me with her to the grocery store. Mom told me years later that I yelled across the store, "John Conrad, my friend." In a time and place not usually welcoming to men like John, my mother introduced me to "my friend."

Francine became my friend in Haiti. In February 1982 we lived in Port-au-Prince. After the trek from his home in Dessalines, Francine found our house in the city. As we talked that afternoon I asked him a personal question. "Francine, how do you feel deep in your heart when you see my house with electric lights, a steel gate, and two toilets with water to flush them?"

My thirty-three-year-old friend carefully assured me that he felt no envy. He said, "I don't want this house. I have no money to pay the electric bill each month, and I can't drive a car. I'm happy for you, but I can't use this house or your things."

Then Francine asked me a question. "Can I give you counsel?" He asked for permission to speak from his heart. I quickly agreed to receive his inmost thoughts.

"If I come to see you again and knock on the gate, it's not good if you speak to me through the gate because then the neighbors think I'm a nobody. But if you greet me and bring me inside, if we drink a cold soda together, that's enough. I don't need your big house. I just want to be your friend."

Francine was my friend. James became my friend in Kenya. Wilson became my friend in Uganda. These were my people.

Soon after moving to Kericho, Kenya, Karen invited our neighbors to our house for dinner. That evening O. E. told us that he came from a part of India evangelized in the first century by doubting Thomas. His family had deep roots in the Christian faith. After O. E. graduated from college in India, he went to the United States for graduate study. By the time we met, he had spent about twenty-five years teaching theology to African students.

In 2008, O. E. and Miriam invited us to go with them to southern India to construct a library on the Bible college campus where they had studied more than three decades before. Karen and I saw this as an opportunity to explore more of the world and to engage in God's mission in new ways. We knew of the need for religious books in India, so we put out the word. Retired pastors donated their libraries. People in many congregations cleaned out the bookcases in their houses. We shipped eighteen thousand books to India in a sea-land container. Further, we placed four hundred sewing machines on top of the boxes of books that persons could use for income.

We traveled to India prior to the delivery of the sea-land container. When the container arrived, we began the task of sorting the books by twenty-seven categories. Once we organized the shipment, we invited the professors to select books useful in their departments. The librarians came next to select books to go on the shelves. Persons from other Bible schools and public schools in the area selected books. Pastors stopped by. Students about to graduate were given a small library. Finally, each student could select three books.

Since the library at the Bible college added four thousand books to their collection, we had to put a top shelf on the existing bookcases. That necessitated the construction of two-step stools so students could reach the top shelves. Before we left India, I delighted to walk through the library and see students

231

sitting on one of the stools as they read a book taken off of the top shelf.

When we returned to Florida, Karen and I moved into a rental house. On a Saturday, I built simple shelving in our garage on which to store Christmas decorations. I did not feel well and told Karen that it must be the flu. I took two naps that day.

By early the next morning I lay beside the toilet, vomiting, unable to stand on my own. A friend took us to the hospital about seven o'clock on Sunday morning. Both Karen and I carried hepatitis A home from India. The emergency room doctor immediately recognized that I suffered from acute liver failure. I later heard the story that when the emergency room doctor said that my only chance for survival was a liver transplant, I asked, "Well, what is something like that going to cost?"

"About two hundred thousand dollars," the doctor replied.

Karen said that I looked like I was contemplating my options, then said, "Well, let's go ahead and do it," as if my checking account balance would cover it.

Healthcare workers faxed my medical records from Vero Beach, Florida, to the transplant clinic in Miami. When the word came that the transplant program accepted me, medical technicians transported me to Miami where the hospital staff began preparing me for surgery if a donor liver became available. The first couple of days they worked to stabilize me as much as they could. During that week I complained that everyone looked orange, then I thought they all looked green. My body was messed up.

I remember feeling claustrophobic. All of the machines to which I was attached kept me pinned in the bed. I may not have had the strength to do much anyway, but I felt closed off in a tight place. My lower body filled with fluid. Once I was back on my feet, I lost fifty-five pounds in eight days.

I do not remember much about my first week in the hospital. That may be a good thing. What I know about the week comes mostly from what others have told me since my recovery.

The word came on Thursday that a liver was available, but after starting to prep me for the operation, the surgeons determined that the liver was not suitable. So the wait continued.

Because Karen had hepatitis A, too, she could not visit me in the hospital. Shela and Sher'ri took turns shuttling messages back and forth. Karen lay gravely ill in a hotel room. I lay in a hospital room sustained by medical technology. We both grieved at the thought that one of us might die apart from the other.

On Saturday the word came that a suitable liver was on its way to Miami. The surgeon went to get some rest before the marathon operation while others on the transplant team begin preparing me for surgery. I had been in operating rooms in Haiti and Swaziland, so I was fascinated with the setup in Miami. I counted the ceiling tiles as I lay on the operating table before they put me to sleep. I am not sure if it comforted me in some way, but before the anesthesiologist began sedating me I knew the operating room was exactly twenty-eight feet square. In recovery I asked questions about the equipment I saw in the operating room. This operating room looked very different from the ones where I watched surgeries outside of the United States.

As I came out from under the anesthesia about ten hours after the surgery began, the nurses told me that I spoke to them in Haitian Creole. That may have been related to the fact that the nurses were Haitian and speaking Creole among themselves. In Creole, I told one nurse that I was very hungry and named a Haitian dish I wanted, cornmeal mush with bean sauce on top. "And fix it quickly," I added. Speaking Creole in the recovery room prompted many Haitian nurses to stop at my bedside. We talked about the hospitals I had worked on in Haiti. One of the nurses was a good friend of a man I knew. I almost felt like I was attending a family reunion.

While living in Haiti, Haitians taught me to trust God more fully. One day after someone stole Francine's corn crop about the time it could be harvested, I listened as he declared his confidence that God would provide. We had that conversation in Creole. As I lay in a hospital bed in Miami, speaking Creole with the nurses who cared for me, I remembered what my Haitian friend had taught me. I could trust God completely.

The second day after my surgery, the surgeon stood at the end of my bed with two others from the medical staff. He asked if I was awake and could understand him. I assured him that my mind was clear.

"I've grown very fond of you and your family," the doctor said, "but this is the last day I will see you. This hospital is full of sick people and they need my attention. But you are no longer sick." He paused a moment, then asked, "Did you hear what I just said? You are no longer sick. As soon as you can walk you will be free to leave the hospital. I have seen your lab work and you have a pristine liver that is functioning perfectly. During surgery your liver began to function even while we were finishing the transplantation. Someday you will die, but you will not die because of a bad liver."

I rejoiced with the good news. I did not remember everything that happened in the previous ten days, but I knew I had been close to death. I do remember the deep, deep sense of peace. No fear, just tranquility. I also realized that a grieving family provided me the gift of life. I am grateful.

Two weeks after the liver transplant surgery, I returned to the hospital to have the staples removed from the incision. I lay on my back as a doctor took them out, one by one. When just a few remained, he stepped back and said, "I know who you are. You are the man who got sick in India and yet you are not angry with the Indian people." This doctor went on to tell me that he had been on vacation when I received the liver transplant, but others on the medical staff told him my story.

As I thought about the doctor's statement, I failed to understand why he assumed that I would be angry with Indian people because I contracted hepatitis A in India. I still highly respect our Indian friends who invited us to take this trip. I have cherished memories of my Indian friends in Kericho. Even today, hepatitis is not the first thing that comes to mind when I think of India.

Nor do I have bad feelings toward the British doctor in Kampala who treated me for bilharzias. On several occasions when I lived in Uganda, I went by boat from Jenja out into Lake Victoria to build a school on an island. Very poor people live on the island and they manage to survive by fishing and cutting firewood that they transport to the mainland. On one of these trips I became infected with bilharzias, a parasite that attacks the liver. Somehow I was exposed to the parasite in contaminated water. The medicine a British doctor gave me caused me to vomit. My throat felt like it was on fire or that I had been drinking some toxic chemical. Doctors in the Miami transplant unit suspect that the medicine given me at that time probably caused liver damage, which made an infection with hepatitis A lethal for me.

My experience with liver failure and transplant is just a fact. I do not believe that it is good or bad, it just is. God did not judge me or strike me down. No one needs to be held accountable for my ailment. The sudden change in my health altered the course of my life, but even that is okay with me.

I once heard James Ouma pray for God to graciously grant "temporary healing." After the prayer I asked James about his statement. "Jesus provided only temporary healing for those we read about in the Bible," James said. "Everyone that Jesus healed eventually died." James prayed for me when I suffered with bilharzias. Karen had traveled to the United States and James took care of me when I was gravely ill. God answered his prayer and I regained my health, but only for a while.

When the word went out of my liver failure, people around the world started praying. The response of God's people brought strength and courage in challenging days. Friends thoroughly cleaned our house before others drove us home from Miami. When we arrived, a longtime friend waited for us. She came from Alabama to care for us for three weeks. A woman who had been a teenager on the Teen Mission team in 1978 came from Pennsylvania and cared for us for six weeks. When she left, we were well enough to manage on our own.

When I could, I started volunteering with organ donor drives to encourage others to sign up. We went to churches, shopping centers, and hospitals to talk with people about registering as organ donors.

After the transplant, when I could get around on my own, I went to the motor vehicles office to change the address on my driver's license. This was one of those busy offices where you take a number and wait your turn. When I finally made it to the counter, a big fellow was talking with the clerk next to me. I overheard that he had just moved from New York. The clerk asked if he wanted to indicate on his driver's license that he was an organ donor. The man said no.

I looked over at the man. He was as big as a side-by-side refrigerator. He wore a tank top that revealed big muscles. On an impulse, I stepped over to the man and placed my hand on his back. "Please, please reconsider," I said. "You see, sir, I just had a liver transplant. If someone had not been a donor I would not be alive today. We need people like you to be donors. Will you please reconsider?"

The clerk behind the counter looked at me, then at the man. For a moment we all stood in an awkward silence. Then the man from New York said, "Okay, sign me up."

All three of us laughed as the tension broke. The clerk behind the counter said to me, "You need to park yourself right there every day. Together we could sign up a bunch of people."

I happened to be at Missionary Flights (MFI) on the afternoon of January 12, 2010, when news came in about five o'clock that Haiti had experienced a devastating earthquake. The MFI staff met briefly, and then started what would become an intense two-month relief effort. Everyone knew that the MFI planes would fly the next day, so we started moving water filters, blue plastic tarps, and other supplies out of storage. What developed in the next few hours was purely spontaneous, but it looked like we had rehearsed every move.

In the weeks that followed, the twenty-eight-thousand-square-foot hanger was busy from four in the morning to ten at night. Some MFI personnel worked sixteen to eighteen hours, then slept in a motor home in the parking lot. This cycle went on day after day. Volunteers flooded the hanger to pack boxes by day. When planes returned in the late afternoon, the loading for the next day's flights began.

People started dropping off donations. Individuals went shopping and brought in new items. Medical supply companies sent truck loads to be flown into Haiti. A local fruit packing company opened a warehouse to help MFI manage the huge response of compassion.

Karen started the morning after the earthquake assisting with meal preparation. Relief workers flying in and out of Haiti were fed, as were volunteers sorting and packing the supplies donated to the cause. Local congregations signed up for specific meals. A local orange grower arrived with a truck load of fruit. Professional caterers set up serving lines as their contribution to the effort. With so many moving pieces, I marveled at how smoothly things worked in those days.

My primary job involved driving the forklift. I first drove a forklift working at a cherry processing plant while in high school. I had taken a class after moving to Florida and was a certified forklift operator. When loading a C-130, for example, we needed to do so as quickly as possible. When a pallet was ready, I picked it up and transported it to the staging area. For the C-130 we positioned about ninety pallets in a three-wide-by-thirty-long layout so we could quickly load the plane when it arrived.

I was asked to go to Port-au-Prince to assist with the unloading of the relief planes. With numerous agencies sending planes and the limited airport space, the relief effort managers wanted to make the unloading more efficient. They needed a forklift driver, so they asked me. The fact that I speak Creole was a bonus. I would live at the airport. I really wanted to respond to this call, but in the end I said no. Both Karen and I were doing well physically, but I did not want to leave her at this time. I had concerns about what my body might do if I contracted malaria or an infection. I would eventually return to Haiti, but I could not in 2010.

One day I noticed a man sitting alone in the MFI hanger. I went over to speak with him. Hesitantly, he told me his story. He called himself a "machine operator." A relief agency knew of his skills and called him for a specific assignment. That day he waited for an airplane to take him to Haiti. He had been briefed on what he would see and what he would do. He agreed to drive the tractor, a front loader. Workers would place bodies in the bucket that he would lift into dump trucks for transport to mass graves outside of Port-au-Prince. More than two hundred thirty thousand people died because of this earthquake. This man looked like a Midwest farmer. I am not sure what equipped him for this difficult task, except his willingness to suffer with the people of Haiti. Again and again he said, "Someone needs to do it." I prayed for this man often.

As Karen and I look back on our involvement in the Haiti earthquake relief effort, we both think that the long days pushed us toward full recovery from our liver ailments. We confirmed that we had regained physical health. We rejoiced that once again we could play a role in relieving the suffering of others. It was so much fun playing on the winning team! We were part of an effort that packed over four hundred fifty tons of relief supplies and assisted with the shipment of over one thousand tons. Our roles were different than at other times in our life, but we were still in the game.

I have learned a great deal about the function of the liver since receiving the transplant. The liver serves the body as both an organ and a gland. Of the five hundred or so functions of the liver, many can be understood as accessory to other bodily functions: the liver provides bile to assist with digestion, stores nutrients until other parts of the body need them, and regulates the composition of the blood that feeds the cells. My liver transplant provides an image that, to a degree, summarizes my life in that I have most often served as an accessory to the work of others. I constructed hospitals so medical personnel could be more effective. I built schools so teachers would have an educationally rich environment. I put up church buildings so congregations could gather to be strengthened as followers of Christ.

Further, because I worked in cross-cultural contexts, I felt like a transplant on occasion. Sometimes the fact that I was a foreigner became more evident than others. I will be on medicines the rest of my life to prevent my body from rejecting the "foreign" tissue implanted in my abdomen. In a similar way, I had to seek new ways of thinking intentionally, approach issues from new starting places, and learn new methods. Diligently, I had to do the deliberate work of making a home in a place where I did not look like the others around me.

While recovering from the liver transplant, I had plenty of time to think. I am not exactly sure why, but from the first surgeries I observed in Haiti I have been fascinated with the fact that race is not a factor in many medical procedures. I donated blood for the Haitian woman, the bag still warm from the freshly drawn blood as they wheeled her into the operating room. My friend had the exact blood type needed to save the life of a Swazi newborn. The doctor who founded Tenwek Hospital told me that the first blood transfusion at the hospital required three units that came from a Kipsigis Kenyan, an Indian, and a European American. I had been a regular blood donor as a young adult, earning a Gallon Pin award. For years I had been a giver; during the transplant I received the gifts of others. I wondered who my donors might have been. Could persons of other races have prolonged my life?

My early attempts to communicate with the family of the liver donor did not result in a response, but I continued to speculate about the person whose death made my continued life possible. I wondered if a black person might have been my donor. In a sense it seemed to me that if true it would honor the deep connection I have with my friends in Haiti, Kenya, and Uganda. By this time I knew from the work I had done trying to get people to register as organ donors that historically African Americans donate organs at a lower rate than those of European descent. But still that thought came to mind, so I told Karen, "I wish I'd find out that my donor was a black person."

Turns out, my wish came true.

Chapter 24

A Big Brush

Old men sit in the shade because they
planted a tree many years before.

~ Ugandan Proverb

During the time we lived in Kenya, we traveled to Uganda with three missionaries to do some white-water rafting on the Nile River. After lunch on the day we spent on the river, we crossed over the last of the grade five rapids and sat back to enjoy the equatorial sun. When we approached a whirlpool, the guide said that anyone who wanted to could jump into the giant "toilet bowl" and be flushed out downriver. I leaped into the water. I looked over my shoulder and realized no one else took the challenge. I was on my own.

As I swam closer to the whirlpool, I felt the pull of the water. It squeezed my legs. I raised my arms like the guide instructed me to do. Karen said that the last she saw of me were my hands spinning like a pinwheel. The power of the water pulled me under for about twenty seconds, and then coughed me up quite a ways from the rubber raft. When my head popped out of the water, I felt dizzy.

My experience with this whirlpool matched exactly what the guide said would happen. I trusted him and took the plunge. In a similar way, I trusted God. I often felt like circumstances buried me in powerful currents, but I learned that eventually I popped up downstream. Over time I learned to rest in the reality of God's constant presence and provision.

I found reading the Bible each day to be an essential discipline in a life that could be quite chaotic. In the scriptures I found guidance and direction. I began to see more clearly than ever before that only through regular immersion in God's word could a person begin to discern God's way in specific situations.

At the Teen Mission boot camp, we learned that every day each team member would spend thirty minutes in Bible reading. Just the Bible; no other devotional material could be used during that period. Everything else stopped so each person could find a quiet, private place to read and reflect on the scriptures.

As the Teen Mission team director, I led by example. A marvelous thing happened that summer that continued in the years that followed. From Genesis through Revelation I began to see God on a mission to save the world from sin and the consequences of sin (emphasis added):

Genesis 12:1–3: Now the Lord said to Abram, "Go from your country and your kindred and your father's house to the land that I will show you. I will make of you a great nation, and I will bless you, and make your name great, so that you will be a blessing. I will bless those who bless you, and the one who curses you I will curse; and <u>in you all the families of the earth shall be blessed</u>."

Revelation 7:9–10: After this I looked, and there was a great multitude that no one could count, <u>from every nation, from all tribes and peoples and languages</u>, standing before the *throne and before the Lamb, robed in white, with palm branches in their hands. They cried out in a loud voice, saying, "Salvation belongs to our God who is seated on the throne, and to the Lamb!"*

I had heard sermons on the Great Commission (Matt. 28:18–20), but for the first time I realized that God's desire that disciples come from all nations did not begin just before Jesus ascended into heaven. From beginning to end, I started to see, the Bible is about God on a mission.

I began writing in the margins of my Bible. I used "GC" as an abbreviation for the Great Commission to note those passages that showed God's mission. As days evolved into weeks, I started to list key words and phrases in the front pages of my Bible. When I looked at my notes, I realized that God has always been seeking those who need life. When I saw God in this new way, I began to see myself in new ways too. If God is about serving those who walk in darkness, those who are lost, those who are broken, then I, too, must do the same if I am to be a faithful disciple of Jesus.

My prayers changed. On the nights in Dessalines when the Vodou priest whipped the people into a frenzy, I often stood in the darkness in my boxer shorts and slippers and watched. I witnessed the power of evil. I wept as I watched some of the men who worked on the hospital construction crew intoxicated and frantic in their search for peace. I prayed for the Holy Spirit to drive out the evil spirits. I prayed that I might be a light in the darkness.

When children came close to me in Haiti, I often reached out and touched them. As I gently patted a child's head or shoulder, often for only a moment, I prayed for the child. I prayed for God's protection over the little girls. I knew the sexual exploitation many would have to endure. I prayed for God's guidance for the little boys. The Bible made it clear that

God cared for these children. My Bible reading helped me pray for the people around me in new ways.

Over time, I began noticing that solutions to the dilemmas I faced came in the early mornings. As I began the morning in prayer, even as I still lay in my bed, ideas came to mind. Construction methods in rural Kenya were far from what a builder would do in the United States. At times I had to forget the U. S. building codes, OSHA regulations, American building materials, and specialized tools. The American way of thinking about construction could take me only so far. Often the Holy Spirit became my teacher and guide as I ventured into new situations with challenges I could not anticipate.

I changed. After living in Haiti, I was a different person. I do not know how else to express it than to say that the old had gone and the new had come. I saw the pervasive nature of God's mission in the Bible. I believed that to be a faithful follower of Christ, I needed to join God's mission with my whole being. My family joined me in fully engaging ourselves in that mission no matter where it took us, no matter what it cost us, no matter how it inconvenienced us. We were fully devoted. We were energized. We were zealous.

But then we returned to the United States.

A pastor of a large church invited me to speak about the project in southern Mexico. I left work early on a Wednesday afternoon and drove a couple of hours to speak to his congregation. I went optimistic that from this congregation we would sign up short-term mission team members and raise money for materials. We enjoyed a fine meal and good fellowship before I spoke. At the end of the evening, the pastor urged the congregation to give enough that they could pay my gas expenses for the day. *Gas money?! That is it?* I drove home unable to explain the disconnect between what I expected as a response from this congregation and what the pastor allowed. It seemed to me that this pastor felt like his congregation needed to hear stories about engaging in the Great Commission, but he did not really want his people to do so directly.

When I urged one pastor to involve the congregation in Great Commission action more fully, he explained that the church finances "pie" was being cut into smaller pieces. With the high mortgage payments, he said, they could only do a limited amount for the global mission. So I suggested that the mortgage be paid off. I had estimated the value of the cars in the parking lot; the total exceeded the balance of the mortgage.

"Swanee, Swanee," the pastor said, "you surely know those cars are not paid for."

"The banks think they *will* be paid for," I replied. "These people have the financial wherewithal to do that. If they can afford to make car payments, this congregation can pay off the church debt that keeps them from fully engaging in the Great Commission."

My words had no impact. My logic seemed foolish to this pastor. I felt like some people considered me a naïve teenager who did not (and probably could not) understand the complexity of American Christianity. My idealism should be tolerated, they implied, but ultimately ignored. Maybe after I passed through my adolescent phase I would get it.

I admit I did not understand. I did not understand why the pragmatics of running a religious enterprise exempted the American church from participation in God's global mission. I did not understand how persons with more theological sophistication than I had could seemingly miss that God's mission ran from the beginning to the end of the Bible like veins of gold just waiting to be mined. I did not get it then, and I do not get it now.

I started paying attention to numbers. Only about five percent of the world's population lives in the United States. My focus shifted to the ninety-five percent. I estimated that it took ten dollars to build a church in the United States compared with the one dollar it took in Haiti. I began to invest my money where it went further. I carefully studied *Operation World* by Patrick Johnstone and noted those areas of the world that seemed responsive to the gospel. I liked reading Johnstone's book better than flipping through a tool catalog! I started thinking about where in the world I could go; I wanted to be where mission effectiveness would be the greatest.

I found myself in a place I never expected to be. I was a citizen of the United States. My church membership was with an American congregation. But I felt out of place. This did not seem like home anymore. These people I had known for decades, my church family, began to feel distant from what I had come to value as essential to my understanding of the Christian life.

I grieved for the American church. I grieved for congregations that poured millions of dollars into buildings for Sunday events. I grieved over self-help sermons that put a spiritual veneer over materialism and narcissism. I grieved over power dynamics within the church that shut out the most vibrant Christians in the world in favor of the few with the most money. I grieved over lies and sins swept under the carpet to protect a few "godly" people in positions of power. I grieved over organizational policies so tightly drawn that most persons were filtered out of responding to God's call. I grieved that global missions was seen as "old school," the kind of things our grandparents did, and not worthy of attention given the new way of doing church in the United States.

I failed to communicate my grievances well. The disconnect I saw between what I found in the Bible about God's mission and what I saw in the American church distressed me. I tried to tell others about what I saw. I wrote letters. I had to-the-point conversations. Too often, I widened the gap between those I so desperately wanted to influence and myself. I am sorry for that.

Friends took me aside and spoke words of caution. They advised me to avoid the risks they saw in my actions and dreams. Numerous times someone told us that they could never do what we had done. "We have a close family," they said. The implication was that Karen and I could move to Africa because we did not have good family relationships. But they did not see my father wrap his arms around me in a bear hug and weep as Karen and I prepared to go. They did not see my tears at the airport in Boise as we left our oldest daughter when we returned to Haiti to build the hospital at Dessalines. We, too, had strong family ties. Karen grieved greatly when she could not attend the funeral for her sister. I listened to the words of caution from my friends, but that did little to resolve the disparity that seemed so clear to me between the worldwide reach of God's mission and the shortsighted nature of the evangelical church in my homeland.

Some people urged me to measure my words, to speak more gently. I knew I failed to communicate well, but that did not erase the problem I saw. In some instances, I just stopped talking. I never considered myself a prophet, but I think I know what Jesus meant when he said that "no prophet is accepted in the prophet's hometown" (Luke 4:24). My longtime friends did not want to hear me talk about what I had learned through Bible study, prayer, and experiences in other countries, so we just talked about other things. The most important things in my life as a Christian could not be discussed.

I had *some* hope for the American church, and maybe that kept me trying when it seemed like someone might listen. I knew that some congregations responded well to the Great Commission. In our early days in Haiti, a young missionary friend told me that he and his family were returning to the United States to touch base with their prayer partners.

When I said something about doing a lot of travel, going from church to church for deputation services, my friend told me that he would only visit with his home congregation. Then he described how this congregation of about one hundred fifty members sent five families to other countries as missionaries. This congregation understood the Great Commission and financially supported five persons (and their families) who had grown up in their youth group. These people got it; they understood their responsibility to fully engage in God's mission for the sake of the whole world. I rejoiced when I heard this story.

But that was not the response of some of my friends. I grieved when I thought about those who resisted this type of involvement in God's mission. Maybe they just did not realize how bad things were in other parts of the world.

But I knew. And I had a responsibility to do what I could. "Rescue those who are unjustly sentenced to death; don't stand back and let them die. Don't try to disclaim responsibility by saying you didn't know about it. For God, who knows all hearts, knows yours, and he knows you knew! And he will reward everyone according to his deeds" (Prov. 24:11–12 TLB).

Feeling less at home in the United States made it easier to go as doors opened elsewhere. The issue for me was "where," not "if." When I started this journey while in my mid-thirties, I looked for a missionary position with a salary, housing, and respect within a fine organization. Later, Karen and I just wanted to serve. We would pay our own way if necessary and follow the call from wherever it came. We stayed plenty busy with that approach.

I heard someone say that God paints with a big brush. As a carpenter, that image stuck with me. Finding God's will was easy, I discovered, because of the big brush. I did not have to search for the tiny brush strokes. God is on a mission to bring reconciliation to the whole world and God has invited us to join that mission. God's gracious action swirls all around us; we just need to jump in the current of God's Spirit. I came to the point where I stopped looking for God's will and I started doing the obvious thing right in front of me. I just began to live in ways that I found described in the Bible, to care for the children, to comfort those who suffer, to provide what I could to those in need. Living God's way is not complicated.

Over time I became more comfortable with the fact that we never could see the end from our vantage point at the beginning. When we prepared to move to Kericho, Kenya, one day I walked into the garage where Karen sat on the floor packing boxes. "I feel like Mrs. Abraham," she said. *Oh, no, I thought, she's pregnant.* She went on to say, "It's difficult to pack without knowing where or how we will live." I know that feeling, and it eventually felt okay. With the one hundred twenty-five church roofs we installed in Kenya, we never had all of the money we needed before we started the building process. Sometimes we let a project "rest" while we waited for necessary funds to come in, but in the process I learned to trust in God's timing.

We had just finished putting on the roof for a rural congregation in Kenya. The job had been a challenge since the people had collected four types of metal roofing that did not interface easily. We struggled to make the various types work together, but we eventually got it done. When we finished the last task, we wanted to get started on the drive home since dark clouds indicated rain and the roads were already in bad shape. When the elderly pastor and his congregation urged us to join them for a brief service of thanksgiving, we delayed our departure. The church building was about half full when the pastor began to speak.

This tall, old man described how an older man, three older women, and he began the construction of their church building. These five feeble people dug the footings and carried

249

the stones for the foundation of a church building about twenty-eight by forty feet. Neighbors laughed at them, but they persisted. Three years from the time they started, we put on the roof.

I watched as the pastor's oldest daughter hugged her father as he told this story. I suspect that they sometimes wondered if they would ever finish the building. The pastor had cancer, so they likely considered if he would live long enough to see the dream come true. I can imagine the prayers for God to make a way when the situation looked impossible. In the end, they got it done. The skeptics were wrong. God answered their prayers.

Karen and I became part of God's answer to this elderly pastor's prayer. I can think of no privilege as fulfilling as participating in God's mission and becoming an answer to prayer.

When I look back over our lives, I see time after time when God brought comfort through our care, when God spoke through our words of encouragement, when God defended the oppressed through our actions. We did not necessarily recognize it at the time because we simply tried to be faithful, to do what needed to be done next. We had no master plan, no blueprint, just the quiet confidence that God was out in front and inviting us to take another step faith, to go as a way opened.

Now to him who by the power at work within us is able to accomplish abundantly far more than all we can ask or imagine, to him be glory in the church and in Christ Jesus to all generations, forever and ever. Amen (Eph. 3:20–21).

About the Authors

M. L. "SWANEE" SCHWANZ lived outside of the United States for almost twenty years and assisted with the construction of about 250 hospitals, schools, and churches in eleven countries. He designed a roof truss system currently used by numerous mission agencies and has served as a consultant for campus design and electrical, water, and sewer system installation. He founded GAP International in 1992 to partner with Christian agencies for construction projects, relief and development initiatives, pastoral education, and orphan care. Swanee currently serves as the chair of the International Outreach committee at Christ Church Vero Beach and as a volunteer with Missionary Flights International and Indian River Habitat for Humanity. He previously served on church boards and as an elected delegate to the Church of the Nazarene General Missions Convention and General Assembly. He and his wife Karen live in Florida, are the parents of two adult children, and grandparents to six grandchildren.

KEITH SCHWANZ has served as a pastor, church musician, and seminary educator. He now works as a writer, ghostwriter, editor, and publisher. Keith co-authored the book *Marks of the Missional Church: Ecclesial Practices for the Sake of the World*, the winner of the 2015 Illumination Book Award in the ministry/ mission category. In 2013, he participated on the Midwest Voices panel and provided op-ed columns for the *Kansas City Star*. He and his wife Judi live in Kansas, are the parents of two adult children, and Papa and Nana to six grandchildren.

CPSIA information can be obtained
at www.ICGtesting.com
Printed in the USA
FSOW02n0706050615
7652FS